INVESTING THROUGH YOUR BUILDING YEARS

INVESTING THROUGH YOUR BUILDING YEARS

LARRY BURKETT

VICTOR BOOKS

A DIVISION OF SCRIPTURE PRESS PUBLICATIONS INC.
USA CANADA ENGLAND

Portions of this book were adapted from *The Complete Financial Guide for Young Couples*

All Scripture quotations are from the *New American Standard Bible,* © the Lockman Foundation 1960, 1962, 1963, 1968, 1971, 1972, 1973, 1975, 1977.

Editors: Adeline Griffith, Greg Clouse, Ron Durham
Cover Designer: Joe DeLeon
Cover Photo: Comstock

Library of Congress Cataloging-in-Publication Data

Burkett, Larry.
    Investing through your building years / Larry Burkett.
       p.   cm.
    ISBN 1-56476-097-9
    1. Investments — Religious aspects — Christianity.
    2. Finance, Personal — Religious aspects — Christianity.
    3. Christians — Finance, Personal. I. Title.
    HG4521.B79   1993
    332.024'01 — dc20   92-40975
                                        CIP

CONTENTS

INTRODUCTION   7

1 WHY INVEST?   **9**

2 CRITICAL FACTORS   **17**

3 SPECIAL CONCERNS FOR 20S TO 40S   **35**

4 THE WORST INVESTMENTS   **54**

5 THE BEST INVESTMENTS   **77**

6 THE FIVE-TIER SYSTEM   **92**

7 EVALUATING INVESTMENTS   **107**

8 FOLLOWING SOLOMON'S ADVICE   **131**

GLOSSARY   **145**

INTRODUCTION

The typical financial logic in our generation says that a young couple should buy a home (usually based on two incomes), open an IRA to shelter some income, and start a savings plan for the children. In addition they are told they need all kinds of insurance (life, disability, liability). I believe that logic is faulty. There are specific goals that should be met at each phase of life, not simultaneously.

Let's assume that one goal is to own a home debt-free; a second is to provide adequately for your family in the event of premature death; a third is to have enough surplus to help your children with college expenses; and a fourth is to be able to give at least 20 percent of your income to the Lord's work—and all this by age 40. If you achieve all these goals, you'll be in the 3 percent of Americans who have.

Investment is anything but an exact science, as anyone who has ever lost money on a "sure thing" can testify. But there are basic rules that apply to investing, just as there are basic rules for physics. For example, the law of gravity says that an object will be drawn toward another object of greater mass. Thus when you jump in the air you ultimately come back down to earth. If you fill a balloon with helium, it will seemingly defeat the law of gravity, but only until the helium leaks out; then it will return to earth again.

Investing's law of risk and return works the same

way. The higher the promised rate of return, the higher the risk of losing your money. Economic upturns and inflationary markets can temporarily make that law seem defeatable, but eventually the market deflates and the high-return investments plummet to earth again, along with your hard-earned savings. So an overview of the economy reveals how it affects investment strategies.

Then a basic overview of what God's Word has to say about investing throws further light on the subject. The rules from God's Word about investing still work. Apply them and you will prosper over the long run. Violate them and you will lose all that you have worked so hard to accumulate.

Good reading, God bless you, and I trust you will decide this book has been a good investment.

1

Why Invest?

I once was challenged by a dedicated Christian who was convinced that storing assets for the future was contrary to God's will. We do have the Parable of the Rich Fool in Luke 12:16-21, which warns against storing up material goods for the self while not endeavoring to be "rich toward God." But this just teaches against self-centeredness and greed, not against meeting legitimate needs.

BIBLICAL REASONS FOR INVESTING
The Bible gives several very good reasons for saving and investing, while issuing several warnings against doing so for the wrong motives.

In Praise of Industry

Solomon said, "Go to the ant, O sluggard, observe her ways and be wise, which having no chief, officer or ruler, prepares her food in the summer, and gathers her provision in the harvest" (Proverbs 6:6-8).

Most people at age 25 are thinking about how to buy their first home, pay off their school debts, and find the "right" job. Few are really interested in what investments have the highest rates of return with the least risk. That's both understandable and normal. Remember that *investing for the future is inversely related to spending during the present.*

To Give to Others

The Parable of the Talents (Luke 19:12-26) is a clear mandate to use what God gives us — including money — in a way that earns Him a good return on His investment. The key is to be good stewards for the glory of God, and not ourselves.

The Apostle Paul directed the Corinthians to save in order to give (1 Corinthians 16:1-2). Investing wisely allows you to do this kind of giving. If the church itself is ever to break out of the borrowing habit, then Christians who invest must maintain some surpluses and be willing to give to meet legitimate needs.

Providing for Our Own

The Bible also teaches that we are to provide for our own — we who do not are "worse than unbelievers" (1 Timothy 5:8). The loving father in the Parable of the

Prodigal Son obviously had a surplus that he was storing for his sons (Luke 15:11-24). And in 2 Corinthians 12:14 Paul stated an accepted doctrine in his own day that is equally true today: parents should provide for their children.

WRONG MOTIVES

Actually, in my experience not many Christians who engage in *speculative* investing do so for the right reasons. Too often lesser motives interfere.

Greed

It is very easy to rationalize greed. If you save and invest merely to gain wealth, no amount will ever be enough. For Howard Hughes, $2 billion wasn't enough. For Donald Trump, $1 billion was too little. It is important that we realize the truth of Ecclesiastes 5:10: "He who loves money will not be satisfied with money; nor he who loves abundance, with its income."

It has been my observation that those who lose the most money in investments do so because of greed. That is what motivates high-income professionals to risk money in abusive tax shelters. Most could pay their taxes and still have plenty to live on comfortably. But the desire to hang on to a little more tempts them to take excessive risks.

Slothfulness

It may seem strange to say that slothfulness is a motive for investing, but it is. If you fail to plan well and discipline yourself during the ages of 20 to 40, you may be tempted to panic later when you are faced with such expenses as a college education for your children. This sometimes results in making high-risk investments — to make up quickly for the years when you lacked foresight and industry. As Proverbs 20:4 says, "The sluggard does not plow after the autumn, so he begs during the harvest and has nothing."

Ego

Many people, Christians included, invest to bolster their pride. Why would a wealthy Texas oil family, worth somewhere between $4 and $7 billion, lose everything while trying to corner the silver market? Certainly not because they needed more money. The motive in such cases can be sheer ego and the drive to have more than others. But as Proverbs 29:23 says, "A man's pride will bring him low, but a humble spirit will obtain honor."

The Game of It

To some people, making money is simply a game, and their ego drives them to win. It can become an addiction as serious as alcohol or drugs. Everybody and everything become pawns in the game: family, friends, even God. But the wise man counsels: "Better is the poor who walks in his integrity than he who is crooked though he be rich" (Proverbs 28:6).

All this is a reminder that *we should set our financial goals and pray about them before attempting to do any investing.* If you or your spouse sense that your motives are anything but biblical, it would be better to give the money away now than risk losing something far more important than money—your relationship with the Lord.

BIBLICAL PRINCIPLES FOR INVESTING

There are approximately 12 basic principles of investing to be found in God's Word. Although we will be referring to most of them at one time or another, I want to address three of them here because they are the ones most frequently violated by investors I have counseled.

Principle #1: Surety

The term "surety" means "to take on contingent liability." The most common example found in the Bible is cosigning for someone else's debts. For example, Proverbs 11:15 says, "He who is surety for a stranger will surely suffer for it, but he who hates going surety is safe."

The logic behind this warning is simple. When you cosign a note held by a third party, you have no control over when it might come due. Even cosigning for someone you know isn't safe; it's broken up many a friendship, since it's like the joke about the definition of a "distant relative"—a close relative who owes you money.

You even sign surety on your own loans when you sign a note payable and do not have a clause guaranteeing that the lender will hold you harmless if you fail to pay the loan off according to the terms of the contract. And since not many lenders will agree to such terms these days, you must be careful not to pledge too many of your assets against each new loan. This is one reason it is dangerous to invest borrowed money.

One Christian investor, whom I'll call Martin, is a sober example. He made his initial fortune in the oil and gas business in Texas and Oklahoma. Then he diversified and expanded into the blossoming real estate market. By the mid-seventies, his personal worth was said to be nearly $50 million.

Then, in 1981, the oil market collapsed, and both oil and real estate prices plummeted. Martin was sure he could ride out the crisis, but he had signed surety on every loan he acquired in recent years. When he borrowed, he pledged everything he had accumulated up to that point to secure the new loan. When many of the nation's savings and loan institutions were shut down by the government, all of Martin's outstanding loans became due and payable.

In 1990 Martin saw his home and cars being auctioned off by a court-appointed administrator. Every asset he owned — even his home — was pledged against every loan he had negotiated.

What a tragic example of the truth of Proverbs 17:18: "A man lacking in sense pledges, and becomes surety in the presence of his neighbor."

Principle #2: Risk
The general rule is: the greater the potential return on an investment, the greater the potential risk. Risk, in

and of itself, is not necessarily bad. Even taking out a certificate of deposit (CD) involves some risk. After all, that's what the free market system is all about. But when the risk goes beyond common sense it is poor stewardship, and losses become the norm.

With few exceptions, those who take excessive risks do so because they lack the knowledge or ability to evaluate the actual risk. As Proverbs 21:5 says, "The plans of the diligent lead surely to advantage, but everyone who is hasty comes surely to poverty."

Just be very certain you know what the actual risk is, and decide if you're willing and able to absorb it if there is a loss. Remember the counsel of Proverbs 27:12: "A prudent man sees evil and hides himself, the naive proceed and pay the penalty."

Principle #3: Diversification

In an ever-changing economy, no one can say with certainty what will be a good investment over the next 10 years and what will be a loser. Over the long run, there are basic areas of investing that do well. These include food, housing, transportation, and health care. But even these areas have gone through major cycles during the twentieth century. An investor who had all of his or her funds in any one area would have found it difficult to survive during a major down cycle without a large cash reserve and very little debt.

The point is, there are no sure things; so diversification is essential to long-term stability. And diversification means more than just splitting your money between stocks and bonds. It means investing in some assets that are "paper," such as stocks or bonds, and some that are real, such as real estate. It also means investing in assets that are not totally dependent on one country's economy: European stocks and bonds, Japanese companies, mortgage loans in the Eastern bloc nations, and so on.

The world's wealthiest man, King Solomon, wrote, "Divide your portion to seven, or even to eight, for you do not know what misfortune may occur on the earth" (Ecclesiastes 11:2). That advice is still as sound today as it was 3,000 years ago. As my grandfather's generation used to say, "Never put all your eggs in one basket."

Critical Factors

There are many strategies for investing; no one of them is better or worse than the others. In great part the strategy you select depends on your goals, your age, your income, and your temperament. Each investor must consider all of these or the result will usually be turmoil, frustration, and financial loss.

It is important to remember that good investment strategy involves a great deal more than just achieving specific goals. It involves factors such as personality and temperament, the age and stage at which you invest, and the amount of funds you want to commit.

Often our personalities and temperaments have flaws that would keep us from achieving God's full potential for our finances. To offset these flaws God, in His infinite wisdom, has given most of us spouses who mirror ourselves. In other words, they are exact opposites. I have said many times what I believe to be absolutely true: If a husband and wife are similar, one of them is unnecessary. In order to reach the proper balance in any investment strategy, it is necessary that spouses communicate regularly about finances. For those who are single through choice, divorce, or a spouse's death, it is important to seek out someone close (who is as opposite as possible) to act as a counselor. One of the ways you can tell when you have found the right person is that he or she is the one individual who never agrees with you.

COMMUNICATIONS FACTOR

With some exceptions men are the primary risk-takers in the area of investments. Perhaps this is by culture, or perhaps it is by temperament, but no matter the reason it is normally so. For instance, a man often looks at a house as a potential source of capital when needed. A woman looks at a house as her home and rarely is willing to risk it unless there is no other choice.

Men are far more subject to get-rich-quick schemes than are women. In fact, of the several hundred schemes I have personally known about, less than 5 percent were promoted or purchased by women. Perhaps this is because women have been conditioned to listen rather than react, and as a result they are better able to hear the Holy Spirit's voice warning them.

This I do know: I have sat across the table from

scores of men who were describing some of the most incredibly stupid investment schemes I had ever heard of, most of which could be eliminated on the basis of common sense. Without any discussion I would often ask the wife, "What do you think about this idea?"

Her response was invariably the same. "I don't know what he's talking about, but I have a real check in my spirit about this."

With no real statistical information the wife usually came to the correct conclusion. It was as if God were saying to her, "Would you please stop this dummy before he loses any more money!"

Interestingly enough, though, if a husband is in financial need because of a bad decision and asks for his wife's help, I find most wives ready and willing to do whatever is necessary, including selling their homes, cars, jewelry, or other prized possessions.

Perhaps the Scripture verse that best describes the relationship that a husband and wife should have in all areas, including investing, is found in Genesis 2:24: "For this cause a man shall leave his father and his mother, and shall cleave to his wife; and they shall become one flesh." The closest translation to "one flesh" we have in our generation is "one person." God desires that a husband and wife function as one person, the strengths of one balancing the weaknesses of the other. One of the biggest mistakes any husband can make is to exclude his "helpmate" from the decision process. The same can be said of a wife, but for a wife to exclude her husband from financial decisions is uncommon.

Unfortunately, many wives don't want to be involved in the financial decisions of their husbands. This is very shortsighted on their part and denies the husband the balance God provides through the marriage relationship. It should also be noted that wives outlive their husbands nearly 85 percent of the time, the average age at which a woman is widowed being under 60 years of age. This means that most wives will end up inheriting their husbands' plans, whether they want to or not.

THE AGE FACTOR

Age is a very critical factor when making investment decisions. The younger you are, the more risk you can take and still recover if you're wrong. A 25-year-old investor can make some mistakes and still have plenty of time to recover. A 75-year-old investor can ill afford any mistakes, assuming he doesn't have an unlimited supply of money.

If you do not violate the principles of leverage and surety, there are virtually no situations from which you cannot recover if you are 40 years of age or less. The most you can lose is the money you have at risk. And assuming you didn't borrow it, you can only lose what you have, not future earnings. Therefore, if you are between 20 and 40 it would be reasonable for you to take more risks than you would take at age 60, assuming you have the temperament to accept some losses.

Several years ago a young man called to ask for counseling. He was interested in investing in commodity option contracts and was trying to do what the Bible admonished in terms of seeking counsel from older Christians.

As you have probably gathered by now, I am not a great advocate of commodities investing since much of it borders on pure gambling. In a conversation over lunch this young man described the research he had done on a particular commodity (wheat) and the prospect of an extremely poor wheat crop in the Soviet Union that year. He was considering buying some options on winter wheat futures. By buying an option his loss would be limited only to the money he had at risk. If the wheat prices went down he could forfeit his option, losing what he had invested to that point but with no contingent liability. If prices went up he could execute his option and sell the wheat or actually resell his option at a profit.

He had saved the money he wanted to risk and had discussed the idea with his wife, who had agreed to support whatever decision he made. They had no children and were renting an apartment. If his "hunch" was right he could make enough money to buy a home for cash, lay aside several thousand dollars for future education needs, and still have several thousand dollars left over.

My question to him was, "If you lost every dime you plan to risk, would you look back with regret?"

He said he had prayed about it and felt he could accept either the loss or gain as the Lord's will.

"What about your wife?" I asked.

"She feels the same way," he replied without hesitation.

"Then go for it," I told him. "If you don't, you may never have this chance again." Upon such opportunities fortunes are made (and lost).

He did purchase the options for winter wheat. That year Russia suffered its largest crop loss in nearly a hundred years. The money he had risked grew by nearly 2,000 percent, at which time he cashed out, paid his tithes and taxes, bought a home for cash, and invested nearly $25,000 in a quality mutual fund for his future children's education. He never repeated the investment risk he took that year, to my knowledge, and settled into a career as a computer programmer. But at 25 he had time to recover, even if he had made a bad guess.

A doctor friend in his mid-thirties had made some poor investments in apartment buildings that created so much stress they nearly wrecked his health and marriage. He correctly observed the principles of debt and surety by investing in limited partnerships that required only the commitment of his initial investment capital. However, the investments had outstanding mortgage loans. Several of the investments failed due to economic circumstances, which created a huge tax liability for him.

So many of the investments he had made through his retirement plan went sour that the IRS did an audit. They determined that many of the loans and investments he had made violated the "prudent man rule" (taking a risk a prudent man would not take). They disallowed his retirement plan, throwing the previously deferred income into his taxable income. He ended up owing the IRS several hundred thousand dollars in taxes and penalties, plus interest.

A later appeal to the tax court overturned the IRS ruling and required only that he repay the retirement plan the lost earnings, which amounted to about $100,000. He also lost about $30,000 in legal and accounting fees.

Actually, this man was extremely fortunate because only about 30 percent of tax court decisions go in favor of the taxpayers. By the time his case reached the court, he was well into his forties and his income had declined substantially due to competition from HMOs in his area. Remember that any time you are using tax-deferred money to invest (whether for retirement, government bonds, or anything else) you are potentially extending the risk into a later time period. By the time your case works its way through the IRS and the courts, if necessary, you may be well past your youth.

THE INCOME FACTOR

It seems to be a human fallacy that the more income people have at their disposal the less cautious they are with it. Some years ago I did an informal survey of some doctors and business owners I knew to determine how many of them had lost money in a bad investment. I was astounded to discover that 100 percent of those surveyed had made at least one bad investment.

Next I surveyed some middle-income families I had counseled and found out that about 50 percent of them had lost money in a bad investment.

Finally, I surveyed average-income families. Of this group about 10 percent had lost money through a bad investment.

The logical conclusion you could draw is that those in the lower income group had less money to risk so they obviously would have made fewer investments. Not so. The percentage of investments made stayed remarkably constant, regardless of the income. But the kinds of investments they chose and risks they assumed changed drastically depending on their incomes.

My conclusion is that the lower income investors are less willing to assume high risks. The higher income investors willingly accept the greater risks. Probably much of this can be explained by what is called "sweat equity." In other words, the lower the income the more sweat went into the money to be risked.

Perhaps the lesson to be learned from this survey is: Treat all of your money as if you earned it chopping firewood for a living.

In spite of all the admonitions in God's Word against excessive risk-taking, I still receive letters from Christians who heard the truth but still violated these basic principles and lost huge amounts of money. I suppose *huge* is a relative term. If you lose all you have, it's a huge amount.

PRINCIPLE #1:
GET RICH QUICK

Proverbs 23:4-5 says, "Do not weary yourself to gain wealth, cease from your consideration of it. When you set your eyes on it, it is gone. For wealth certainly makes itself wings, like an eagle that flies toward the heavens."

I have discussed the issue of "get rich quick" in other books, but I would feel remiss if I didn't cover it again, especially in a book dealing with investments. So for those who have read some of this before, forgive the repetition. For those who have not, please read carefully. This simple discussion can save you much grief and embarrassment.

It continually amazes me how gullible Christians are when it comes to get-rich-quick schemes. With rare exception, virtually all the nationwide get-rich-quick schemes begin inside Christian circles. The only logical conclusion I have been able to draw is that Christians tend to trust one another more than average non-Christians do and therefore are more easily influenced.

Perhaps one additional factor is the fact that we believe in the supernatural and will risk money in investments that require supernatural intervention. It's almost as if the more impossible the investment, the more Christians want to believe in it. This is particularly true where the promoters recite Bible verses to justify their claims.

In 1980, at the height of the Arab oil embargo, I was approached by a well-known Christian leader who told me he had been given a "revelation" from God about how to solve America's oil problems. Intrigued by his apparent sincerity, I agreed to hear his revelation. He and two other members of his leadership flew to Atlanta to present the most fantastic revelation of our generation, if it were true.

It seems that he had been approached by an angel one evening while he was praying and the angel revealed to him where the hidden oil deposits in America were located. This angel had pointed to a spot on a map where the largest oil reserves in the world lay untapped. Since it was in an area where no oil had ever been discovered previously and where the geology did not conform to any patterns established by the petroleum industry, I commented, "That would certainly explain why the oil companies have not located this vast, untapped treasure." They were looking in the "oil patch," and this was definitely not in that area.

When I asked why he felt there was oil in such an unlikely location, his response was, "Because God told me that is where it is." As far as he was concerned, that settled the issue once and for all.

"But how do you know your input is from God?" I asked.

He looked at me as if I were a heretic who had challenged the deity of Christ. "I was praying when God told me this," he said in a commanding tone.

The other two men with him nodded in agreement, certain that all my objections had been satisfied since he had received this revelation while praying. They suffered from a common delusion that prayer in itself has some supernatural meaning or power. Don't misunderstand me. I believe God can and does reveal Himself supernaturally through prayer. But the process of praying is not supernatural — God is.

"What do you need from me?" I asked, realizing

further argument was useless since their minds were made up that this was a vision from God.

"We need $3 million to drill a well in this spot," the pastor replied. "It will be the biggest oil find in the world and will make us independent of imported oil. If you will endorse this project we will be able to raise the development funds."

They had already raised nearly $50,000 from people in their church to do a prospectus and brochures. But raising the rest of the money had proved very difficult.

Since I had made an absolute commitment several years before never to endorse any investment products, this helped to extricate me from an uncomfortable situation. I told them the truth, "I never endorse any financial venture. God has not gifted me to give investment advice."

I also suggested that they retain the counsel of a good securities attorney since they were offering stock in several states and it appeared to me as if they had not completed the necessary registrations.

The pastor replied that their securities registration had been blocked by Satan's forces within the state governments, and they had decided to accept money from people in those states anyway. At that point I backed away from even listening to further discussion on the subject. I believe circumstances sometimes warrant opposing government rules, but only when those rules conflict with the ordinances of God. Such would be the case if witnessing were prohibited by law, if worship of God were restricted, or if babies were being aborted. But certainly securities registration would not fall into that category.

The three men went through with the securities sale and a limited drilling operation, raising nearly $600,000 from Christians who heard about the project. In one instance a pastor from another state told his people they would be failing God if they didn't invest in this oil venture. Several families borrowed against their homes to do so. One 80-year-old couple risked their entire savings in the project.

The hole was dry and all the funds were lost, along with several pastors' credibility. Lawsuits flew like snowflakes as disgruntled Christians sued one another in violation of Paul's teachings in 1 Corinthians 6. The media picked up on the lawsuits because many elderly people had been duped into investing. As a result the cause of Christ was set back in the communities most affected. Ultimately the promoters of the venture — including the pastor — were prosecuted, convicted, and given prison sentences.

These weren't stupid people — neither the promoters nor the investors. Neither were they particularly greedy; although without a doubt, the promised returns influenced their decisions. They simply violated the basic rules that God's Word teaches on "get-rich-quick":

Don't get involved with things you don't understand.
Proverbs 24:3-4 says, "By wisdom a house is built, and by understanding it is established; and by knowledge the rooms are filled with all precious and pleasant riches."

It would be difficult to talk a geologist into an investment like the one I just described. Why? Is it because he's smarter than the average doctor who risks his hard-earned money? No, it is because he has acquired wisdom and judgment in the area of his expertise.

Don't risk money you cannot afford to lose.
Ecclesiastes 5:14 says, "When those riches were lost through a bad investment and he had fathered a son, then there was nothing to support him." Not too long ago I risked a modest amount of money in the stock of a company that had been manufacturing computer disk drives. The company had run into some bad times due to poor management and the stock had fallen from about $20 a share to $1. I had done business with the firm several years earlier when they were the leader in the industry and I felt that perhaps under new management they could recover. So I risked $500 in their stock. I didn't want to lose the money, but I knew I could afford to.

Within one month, the company filed for bankruptcy and my stock was worthless. It was a high-risk venture, but it was not a get-rich-quick scheme. I knew the risk, could absorb the loss, and was willing to take a long-term gain.

The most common source of investment capital for get-rich-quick schemes is borrowed money. When investors risk borrowed money in anything, they are being foolish. When they borrow against their homes and needed savings (education, retirement, children), they are being stupid (in my opinion).

One pastor who invested in the oil exploration scheme I described earlier actually borrowed against his elderly mother's home to do so. That goes beyond ignorance into the realm of stupidity.

Don't make a quick decision.

Psalm 37:7 says, "Rest in the Lord and wait patiently for Him; do not fret because of him who prospers in his way, because of the man who carries out wicked schemes." One of the prime elements of a get-rich-quick scheme is that the promoters want a quick decision. The way this is done is to make a potential investor believe that so many people want in on the deal that they're doing you a favor by giving you the opportunity first.

Usually the initial pitch is that you will get a discount or some other special consideration for getting in early. "But if you delay," the promoter warns, "the opportunity will be lost and you'll be left out."

In truth, there is an advantage in getting into most get-rich-quick schemes early on, because most of them don't survive long. So if you get in early maybe you can "sucker" enough friends in to make some money. But if you have a genuine concern for other people, you should discourage, not encourage, them to invest too.

The vast majority of get-rich-quick schemes are built on a pyramid base. This means that they require an ever-expanding supply of new investors (suckers) in order to sustain them. Usually those who join are given a monetary incentive to sell others on the scheme. If, for instance, you invest $5,000 for the right to sell synthetic oil, you can recoup your "investment" (and then some) by enticing others to do the same. These incentives are offered under the most innocuous of terms, such as "finder's fees," "royalties," and "bonuses." The bottom line is simple: If you are dumb enough to risk your hard-earned money, you must know several people who are dumber than you are.

Even as I write, new schemes are roaring through the Christian community. Some are so implausible that at first glance it's hard to believe any thinking person would respond; but they do. I have long since realized that in the realm of get-rich-quick there are no schemes too ridiculous to believe.

Most get-rich-quick schemes get started with a novel idea and enough biblical jargon to make it sound plausible within the Christian community.

Some time back, a novel get-rich-quick program surfaced in churches around the country. The premise behind this particular scheme was based on making loans without interest: a thoroughly biblical concept taught in the Old Testament. In order to participate in the program, investors had to "contribute" 10 percent of the loan they needed. If, for instance, you needed a $50,000 loan (at no interest) you shelled out $5,000 up front—with no guarantee that you would ever get the loan.

Obviously, with no further elaboration than what I have presented, few people would be gullible enough to "invest" $5,000 with no guarantee of an eventual loan. What made this scheme work was the fact that others were receiving such loans and then telling their friends and families.

Most Christians, if they were honest, could relate similar instances when they have lost money because of trusting a Bible-spouting huckster. The "investments" range from jojoba beans in the desert to gas plasma engines that will run on water. Perhaps the most common revolutionary idea is still the 100-mile-per-gallon carburetor. Every decade or so someone will drag that one out and bilk a lot of people out of their hard-earned money. I have often wondered why the car companies would spend millions to eke out another 3 miles per gallon on new cars when they have this great carburetor sitting in the back room!

PRINCIPLE #2:
WAITING TOO LONG

As I said, risk is often related to time. The principle here is very simple: People who wait too long to invest get panicky and then take excessive risks. One of the primary motivations behind state lotteries is this very mentality. Many people see the lottery as a way to make up for a lack of discipline in their earlier years. So people living on Social Security or welfare try to hit the lottery and win a million dollars (or more). The few who do are presented week in and week out as typical success stories by those promoting the system, giving false hope to those who would rather indulge now and gamble later. Obviously, what lottery promoters don't show are the millions who risk their meager earnings and lose.

PRINCIPLE #3: EXCESSIVE RISKS
THROUGH IGNORANCE

Proverbs 13:15 says, "Good understanding produces favor, but the way of the treacherous is hard." As mentioned earlier, a case can be made that everyone who takes excessive risks with their money suffers from ignorance. But we need to differentiate between doing ignorant things (like playing lotteries or trusting in a get-rich-quick scheme), and being financially ignorant.

There is no dishonor in ignorance, provided you don't choose to display it. I have absolutely no knowledge of brain surgery, nor do I desire any. So I diligently avoid all suggestions that I take a Saturday off from what I do best and perform a brain operation. That obviously sounds ridiculous, but in reality that is precisely what many brain surgeons do when they risk months, or even years, of earnings in a shopping center development with no more knowledge of that specialty than I have of brain surgery.

Recently I received a letter from an elderly couple. It seems they had retired from teaching and both elected to take their retirement savings in a lump sum, rather than take a lifetime annuity. This decision was based on the counsel of a financial planner in their church.

The annuities would have paid them a monthly income of about $600 each, which they calculated to be just barely enough to live on. Their lump sum settlement was nearly $200,000. The financial planner told them (correctly) that the lump sum could be invested safely and earn at least $1,500 a month. The additional $300 per month would mean the difference between being able to travel a little versus just paying the bills. So they took the lump sum and rolled it over into an IRA account at the savings and loan where the counselor worked. But instead of investing it in an insured account that would have been covered by the FSLIC (later the FDIC), they invested it in a bond issued by the savings and loan because it had a 2 percent higher rate of return, which amounted to nearly $300 a month more income.

Unfortunately, the S&L (savings and loan) failed and was liquidated by the FDIC within six months of the couple's retirement. The insured accounts were covered by the FDIC, and although it took some months to get all the accounts repaid, no depositors' money was lost. But the bonds issued by the S&L were not insured since they were a debt of the corporation, not the FDIC. The corporation had no assets after liquidation and consequently this couple lost their entire savings.

They took excessive risk because of their ignorance (lack of knowledge). They could have avoided this loss simply by asking any accountant, attorney, or independent financial planner what the actual risk was.

Before you risk money in any investment, first find out what the rules are. Later in this book I'll try to provide the resources you need to evaluate any given investment area.

 3

Special Concerns for 20s to 40s

Many young adults think that everyday living expenses take everything they can make, leaving no room for investments. This is because the average young married couple tries to accumulate in about three years what should take them thirty years to accumulate. The fact is, if you discipline yourself, plan properly, and get your priorities in order, you can begin investing in small ways as soon as you enter the work force, and arrange your finances so that you can invest more later.

Allowing the world to influence the way we handle finances, instead of following biblical principles, has created untold stress on many marriages. Financial pressure from unwisely accumulated debt creates other pressures. A young couple may stop communicating.

They cease to be companions, and become combatants instead. When they talk, it's about financial problems. They don't bother to read their Bibles and pray together any more because it's hard to do this when your mind is consumed with problems. Allow me to illustrate.

A young couple that I'll call Bob and Sue met in college and married when Bob graduated. Sue came from a Christian home and Bob was saved through a campus ministry when he was a college freshman. After college, Bob went to work in a stock brokerage firm and began to do quite well. His first year he made nearly $30,000 in commissions. Consequently, Bob and Sue felt they could commit to buying a home, which they did. Sue's parents loaned them the down payment. With closing costs, attorney fees, and so on, they owed another $1,500, which they charged on credit.

Next came the usual household expenses for drapes, furniture, lawn mower, and appliances. Even so, they might have been able to squeeze by if everything went just right—which it didn't.

Their five-year-old car broke down, as it did regularly, so Bob bought a new car by selling his old car, borrowing some money from his parents, and taking out a $6,000, 18 percent car loan. Although neither Bob nor Sue realized it at the time, they had stepped into one of Satan's modern traps, just as surely as Eve had in the garden. Satan asked Eve, "Indeed has God said, 'You shall not eat from any tree of the garden'?" (Genesis 3:1) Today Satan asks, "Surely you can trust

God for the good things you need, can't you?" And using about the same wisdom as Adam and Eve, Bob and Sue borrowed to buy things they couldn't afford to own. Satan then had them hooked, and all he needed to do was wait until the line played out.

Bob and Sue's line played out when Sue unexpectedly got pregnant about six months after moving into their new home. Frequent bouts of morning sickness caused her to take a leave of absence from her job. Then the downhill financial slide started. Without Sue's income, the house and car payments alone took 70 percent of their pay. After food, gas, utilities, and the other monthly essentials, no money was left for clothes, entertainment, lunches, and least of all, medical expenses.

Every trip to the doctor meant prescription bills and nonreimbursed expenses, and every trip resulted in an argument over money or, more accurately, the lack of it. What should have been a joyful event was soon to be a disaster.

About three months into the pregnancy, the economy soured for stock investing and Bob lost his job. He was out of work for nearly two months, during which time virtually all bills went unpaid. Bob eventually found another job making about $18,000 a year, with a budget that required more than $40,000 just to break even.

Bob and Sue were separated when the baby was born, and she was living with her parents. Bob and Sue had lost their home and their new car and still owed nearly $16,000—all in less than three years of marriage.

Maybe you're thinking, "Well, that won't happen to me," or "It's already too late for us." Neither is true. God's Word has both the prevention and the cure. If you haven't made the errors yet, you have a head start. But even if you have, God's Word offers the absolute cure.

A WORD ABOUT PRIORITIES

The typical financial logic in our generation says that a young couple should buy a home, usually based on two incomes, open an Individual Retirement Account (IRA) to shelter some income, and start a savings plan for the children. In addition they are told they need life insurance, disability insurance, liability insurance, and a good attorney for the divorce that about half of them will face before the seventh year of marriage (because of financial troubles). I believe this logic is faulty. There are specific goals that should be met at each phase of life, not simultaneously.

Let's assume that one goal is to own a home (debt-free); a second is to provide adequately for our families in the event of premature death; a third is to have enough surplus to help our children with college expenses; and a fourth is to be able to give at least 20 percent of our income to the Lord's work: all by the age of 40. There can be some lesser financial goals, but if you achieve these major goals you'll be in the 3 percent of Americans who have.

Most people at age 25 are thinking about how to buy their first home, pay off their school debts, and find the "right" job. Few are really interested in what investments have the highest rates of return with the least risk. That's both understandable and normal. So what I would like to do here is to discuss some ideas that will pay financial dividends later by helping to save money presently. Remember that investing for the future is inversely related to spending during the present.

I would like to begin by working from the smallest to the largest purchases. Attention to the smallest financial details is good training for managing larger amounts of money later.

INSURANCE

We all need some insurance in our modern society, even if it is just liability insurance for our cars or homes. The better you understand exactly what you need, the better decisions you can make. Each dollar not spent on unnecessary insurance is a dollar that can be saved toward long-term goals such as education, retirement, and elimination of debt.

Deductibles

The higher deductibles you can afford, the more you will save on any type of insurance. For instance, if you elect to carry collision insurance on your car the difference between a $100 deductible or a $500 deductible can be as much as half the annual premium. Therefore, if you can absorb the first $500 in repairs you can save

$150 a year or more. The key is to buy only what you need, and not be coerced into a more expensive plan than absolutely necessary. The same can be said for deductibles on home insurance, health insurance, and the like.

Combining Policies

Most people don't realize that by consolidating they can save a considerable amount of money. One company may offer a better rate on car insurance; another may have a better rate on home insurance. But usually one company will write all of your personal property insurance for less than the total of several companies. Also, if you place your property insurance with one company often they will underwrite an "umbrella" liability policy of a million dollars or more for a very small additional cost. You need to ask if this is an option before selecting any company. My insurance company provides me with such a policy and it costs me less than $100 a year extra. This can be an important asset as your financial base grows, especially in our litigating society. One lawsuit, justified or not, can destroy a lifetime of earnings.

I learned with my first home that it is much cheaper to buy my own insurance than to purchase it from the lender. A good homeowner's policy through a reputable company turned out to be less than half the cost of a fire insurance policy sold through the lender. Additionally, a homeowner's policy covers not only the dwelling but contents, liability, jewelry, clothes, and temporary housing.

I also learned that shopping for the best quality insurance at the best price is essential. The cost of insuring personal property will vary by 200 to 300 percent depending on the company you select — so shop. One of the best resources available is the *Consumer Reports* magazine. Each year it evaluates all types of insurance and reports on the liabilities of the country's major insurers. You can normally find a copy of the issue you need at any public library.

Mortgage Insurance
Most mortgage lenders require a mortgage insurance policy that will pay off the outstanding loan balance if a home buyer dies. The mortgage lender often sells an insurance policy costing several times that of an equivalent term life policy from a major insurance company. My advice is to buy your own insurance and assign the amount necessary to pay off the mortgage to the lender. The savings can be significant.

Life Insurance
I can remember being approached by insurance salespeople while in college. They tried to convince me that if I didn't buy right then I might never be insurable again. The truth is, only a small fraction of the population is uninsurable, and most are uninsurable from birth because of diabetes, heart abnormality, or some other congenital disease.

Later I learned that the policies many of these agents offered were inferior, overpriced, and usually blatantly deceptive. Often they were high-cost policies that were heavily financed in the front end to make them appear cheaper. Later the costs rose significantly while the protection declined. In short, they were a rip-off.

Life insurance should be used only to provide for those who are dependent on you while you are living. Otherwise it is a waste of money, in my opinion. If you are not married, or have no children, you rarely need life insurance, except for burial expenses. And if you join a memorial society, they will provide burial services at less than the cost of one year's insurance premium (in most cases).

It has been my observation that the majority of people below the age of 40 who need life insurance are better served with "term" insurance. This is life insurance that accumulates no cash values, pays little or no dividends, and costs a fraction of what a whole life, or cash value, policy costs at the same age. The vast majority of young couples are underinsured and overextended because someone sold them a policy that was too expensive for their needs. A good, annual renewable (to age 100) insurance policy at age 25 to 35 will cost less than one tenth of an equivalent cash value policy at the same age.

If you are disciplined about following the rest of the strategy outlined in this book, your need for life insurance will diminish greatly before the term plan ever reaches the average cost of a typical cash value plan.

A young couple in their twenties can save an average

of $15,000 in premiums before the age of 40 by buying term rather than cash value (whole life) insurance. That money, if invested wisely, will grow to nearly $200,000 by age 65. Let's take a moment to describe the difference between these two kinds of life insurance.

Cash value or whole-life insurance. The huge insurance industry in this country was built on the concept that a fixed annual payment spread out over the anticipated life of the insured would cover both his or her death risk and provide a cash value at the end of the premium-paying period. Because the premiums are amortized throughout this period, they are naturally larger in the insured's younger years because the death risk is less. By investing this overcharge during the early years, the insurance company can offset the cost of paying death benefits in later years.

Some of the newer plans, called "minimum deposit" insurance, require a set amount to be paid into the policy either as a lump sum or over the first few years. Then the deposit is invested and the proceeds are used to maintain the annual payments.

Some insurance companies are "stock companies" owned by investors. The policyholders have no ownership interest in the company. Normally stock companies pay lower returns to the policyholders because of the necessity to pay stockholder dividends, unlike "mutual" companies where each policyholder is a pro-rata owner in the company. In a mutual company, profits are distributed to the policyholders in the form of dividends.

43

Mutual companies were formed to compete directly with the older stock companies. They did so by passing along the profits to their policyholders. This arrangement increased the effective yield of the policies and attracted a large number of participants.

The actual yield to policyholders is often hard to discern because many companies, both mutual and stock, quote their gross yields before all commissions and expenses are taken out. Before investing in any insurance product you need to ask for a detailed analysis of net yield over the previous 10 years.

It is also important to remember that most quoted yields in insurance policies are projected only. They can be changed at any time because of prevailing market conditions, increased company expenses, and even investment losses by the company itself. The only dependable rate is the guaranteed rate, which is normally several percentage points lower than the projected rate.

If you decided to invest in an insurance product, you need to know what it will cost if you elect to drop the plan, withdraw your funds, switch plans, or stop paying any further. You also need to know what the annual fees are, including commissions.

One advantage of cash value or whole life insurance is that the cash value accumulation is not taxable to the insured. As noted earlier, this is because the cash values are really an overcharge of premiums and don't belong to the policy owner but to the insurance company. More recent policies do transfer ownership of the savings to the policy owners at specific intervals or upon the death of the insured.

Term insurance. In the early seventies a new philosophy of insurance emerged: "buy term and invest the difference." The "term only" salespeople simply showed insurance clients how they could buy inexpensive term insurance, invest their savings in other products, primarily mutual funds, and profit greatly. This message reached a new generation who had not experienced the ravages of the Great Depression and were looking for earnings, not security. They bought into the concept of "buy term."

At first the insurance industry tried to ignore the "term" people. But as millions of "whole life" policies were dropped and converted over to term, the industry responded quickly. The result was a new generation of "whole life" products, such as universal life, minimum deposit life, and single premium life. These are actually modified whole life plans that offer higher rates of return for the savings portion of the policy.

In addition, the traditional insurance annuities, or retirement plans, were also upgraded to compete with the skyrocketing mutual fund industry.

In order to offer competitive returns to their policyholders, the insurance companies themselves had to become more competitive by investing their surplus capital at higher rates of return. After all, no company can pay out more than they earn, at least not for long. As a result, many insurance companies now are faced with having many high-risk investments in their own portfolios—junk bonds, commercial loans, and commercial real estate.

It now behooves a prudent investor to evaluate carefully the insurance company that backs the policy he or she owns. Insurance companies are corporations (or associations). As such, the products they sell—life insurance, health insurance, annuities, and so forth—are only as secure as the company themselves.

In order to evaluate an investment in an insurance product, it is necessary to separate the insurance side from the investment side. A number of methods are commonly used to do this. One is to compare the cost of a term insurance policy with that of a whole life policy, less the "investment" side of the latter. The usual method is to use a 10- to 20-year comparison.

For example: Assume you purchased either a $100,000 annual renewable term policy for 30 years (age 35 to 65), or you purchased a $100,000 adjustable life plan at age 35. The adjustable life policy would cost $600 annually, and at age 65 would have accumulated approximately $10,000 in savings.

The annual renewable policy would cost $200 a year at age 35, and increase to $4,300 a year by age 65. Using the early years savings on the term insurance to invest in a mutual fund averaging 10 percent annual growth, the net result at age 65 would be a loss of $3,700.

The difference in cost between term and whole life begins to narrow as your age increases because the annual renewable policy gets progressively more expensive. The only way such a plan will work is to assume you can cancel the annual renewable insurance once your other sources of savings reach $100,000 (or at least reduce the coverage).

The bottom line is: If the total worth of the mutual fund at age 65 is greater than the total worth of the cash value policy, the term is a better investment. If not, the cash value insurance is better. In our example, the latter proved to be better.

This all may sound a little complicated, but any investment advisor or insurance agent with access to a computer can run this comparison for you in a few minutes.

Since I am not trying to sell you anything, I can tell you what I have observed. To date I have not seen any cash value insurance products (universal life, annuities, or other) that would match buying term insurance and investing the difference in a good quality growth mutual fund if the insured was able to shop for a new policy at least every three years. This continually allows for the lowest term rates. But with many of the newer whole life plans, such as adjustable life, the line between insurance and investment tends to blur.

I would also be less than totally honest if I didn't say that only a few people actually buy term and invest the difference. Most buy term and spend the difference. That's okay provided they consciously make that decision, but most simply fail to execute the plans they have made.

Disability Insurance
Disability insurance, outside of a group plan, is generally very expensive if it is designed to provide for a loss

of income for life. The cost is greatly reduced if coverage is reduced. Most younger people would be better off with a plan that provides for three to five years, instead of life. Remember also that Social Security does provide for disability benefits, as does workman's compensation, if the disability is job-related.

Weighing the benefits of disability insurance is critical since the costs are high. Actual costs can vary by 50 percent or more, depending on the company. If funds are limited, disability insurance should be fairly low on your list of priorities. Again, don't be panicked by horror stories of those who failed to carry a disability policy and were permanently disabled. They are the exception to the rule. I would also add that God can still provide, regardless of anyone's disabilities.

CREDIT CARDS

Obviously my advice is don't finance any purchases on your credit cards. The rates are usurious, and the temptation to buy things you don't need and can't afford is amplified by the easy use of credit. If you can't afford to pay cash for consumer items such as food, clothing, vacations, gas, and auto repairs, then do without them. There is no alternative if you ever expect to be financially free. I would refer you to my book, *Debt-Free Living* (Moody Press, 1989) for a complete plan on getting and staying out of debt.

AUTOMOBILES

It is common for most young couples to finance their first car. Unfortunately, many, if not most, opt to buy a car too expensive for their budget and plunge themselves into debt. Pick a car that fits your budget and don't be swayed by advertising that promotes cheap financing. There is no free lunch, and if a company lowers the interest rates to entice you to buy its new car, it's because the car is overpriced.

The least expensive way to finance a car commercially, especially a used car, is often through a credit union. If you are a member of a credit union, explore this alternative first. If you are not, then look for a car that can be paid off totally in two years or less and shop for a simple-interest loan. Stay away from add-on interest loans because they carry a front-end interest penalty if you want to accelerate the payments.

It is usually best not to finance a car loan through a dealer. When you mix trade-ins, finance charges, credit insurance, and sometimes even life insurance, into the deal, it's difficult to tell what the car actually costs. If you have to finance a car, arrange the loan outside and negotiate with the dealer as if you were paying cash — which you are. The convenience of dealer financing is often very costly.

I believe that Christian parents should help their children with their first home and car, if they can afford to do so. Sometimes it is just a matter of asking parents who have the means if they will help. Just be certain that you treat any family loan with the same respect and discipline you would a bank loan. If the parents want to discount the loan, that is their right, not the borrower's.

HOME LOANS

One of the best ways to finance a home is by borrowing funds from a pension or retirement plan. It is possible for anyone to extend a first mortgage loan from his or her retirement account to a nondependent. I personally know many Christians who have done so to help young couples get into their first homes. The obvious advantage is that there are no discount points, closing costs are minimal, and the loan is backed by the home, so the retirement account is protected. Typically the loan is arranged at whatever the prevailing government T-bill rate is, usually 2 to 3 percent less than a commercial loan.

Most home loans today are for 30 years, but just paying an extra $100 a month will retire a $100,000 loan approximately 12 years early and save nearly $140,000 in interest charges that can be used to start a long-term investment program as mentioned earlier.

A second option is owner financing. This is where the person selling the home becomes the lender. Obviously the home must be debt-free for the owner to be able to do this. This is often the best arrangement for both parties. The buyer can arrange a lower interest rate and avoid the discount point penalties normally required by a commercial lender. The seller benefits through the up-front down payment, the home is collateral for the loan, and the interest rate is higher than the prevailing rates they could earn through a bank deposit.

If financing cannot be arranged through a retirement

account or owner financing, shop for the best rate available. Often financing for a shorter period, such as 15 years, can save 1 percent or more in annual interest. On a $100,000 mortgage, 1 percent interest saved amounts to $1,000 the first year.

Government programs at preferred interest rates are often available for first-time home buyers. Since the programs change frequently, you will have to verify them as the need arises.

INVESTMENT GOALS

It is my strong conviction that becoming debt-free, including the home mortgage, should be the first investment goal for any young couple (or person). Once you have achieved that goal, then, and only then, should you invest in other areas. As I said earlier, the exception to this would be a company retirement account with matching company funds from which the proceeds could be withdrawn at some future date to retire a home mortgage.

Let's assume that by the age of 35 you have achieved the goal of becoming debt-free and want to move to the next step, the accumulation of education funds. If the children are within five years of college, at least half of all available funds should be kept in investments that can be converted easily into cash as needed. Normally these will be no-load mutual funds, short-term bonds, or liquid savings plans such as money market funds and CDs.

As the children begin college, the investment plan

can be temporarily curtailed so that current funds can be used for many of the annual expenses. This is really a matter of matching your available funds and costs. The use of local community colleges or state schools can stretch available funds significantly.

Assuming that you have enough surplus funds to meet the need for college, these funds should be accumulated in relatively low-risk investments. Again the prevailing principle is that no greater risks should be assumed than are necessary to meet your goals.

If the funds are insufficient, then higher risks must be assumed. Under any circumstances, the maximum risks that should be taken with designated college funds are probably good quality growth mutual funds. If you can accumulate enough funds to help your children attend a local community college, that is better than to risk everything and not be able to send them at all.

SYSTEMATIC SAVINGS

Perhaps the single most important part of any investment strategy between the ages of 20 and 40 is systematic and regular savings. The temptation, once the home is paid off, is to increase your spending level because the additional funds are available. Most young couples with potential surpluses consume it on bigger houses, cars, boats, motor homes, and vacations. Controlling these indulgences must be a part of your long-term plans.

For instance, if you have a two- or three-step plan to

move up in housing, stick to it. After the third move into the home you have agreed will meet your needs, resist the temptation to move up again. Often to do so will delay your getting debt-free well into your fifties, if ever.

As I said earlier, I prefer mutual funds as a savings vehicle for most people because they will normally accept monthly payments of as little as $10, or as much as you can afford.

Obviously, a reasonable cash reserve should be maintained for emergencies such as layoffs, illness, additional children, and emergency giving. The normal formula for emergency savings is approximately three months of income, although this will vary according to your profession. A postal worker has less need for a large cash reserve than does a real estate agent, by virtue of their respective professions.

If by the age of 40 you have your home debt-free, have saved at least one-half of your first two children's college education expenses, and have begun a long-term investment plan, you will have accomplished more than 95 percent of all Americans today.

 4

The Worst Investments

No one expects you to be an expert on investments in your early adult years. What can be expected is that you try to learn not only what to do but what not to do as well. This chapter deals mostly with observations about bad investments rather than scientific studies. By that I mean I am offering a counselor's view of investments I have seen others make that have lost money consistently. Obviously, there are investment advisors who will disagree with my observations. That's okay too, because I would probably disagree with theirs. The criterion I use here is very simple: Of the people I have known and counseled over the years, which investments made them money and which lost?

Perhaps the simplest, most straightforward method for evaluating any investment is the percentage of people who buy into it and get their money back. The next rule of thumb is how many made a return above their investment. It's very much like evaluating your financial advisor. The rule of thumb is: If he makes you more money than he costs you, he's pretty good.

I have purposely oriented this book toward nonprofessional investors like myself. Even though I am a financial counselor and teacher, I am not a professional investment advisor. The difference between being a counselor and a professional investment advisor is that I don't risk other people's money.

I have always tried to limit my advice to basic financial areas such as budgets, financial goals, and biblical principles. I would personally find it rather hard to sleep at night knowing that I had the responsibility of overseeing the management of other people's money.

Most successful investors are what I call *hedged risk-takers.* By that I mean that they will take risks periodically if they can afford to, but they never take more risks than are considered necessary to accomplish their goals. There are investments that potentially can return great financial rewards, but most are what should be called "sucker bets." (Forgive my use of gambling terms, but that's what most of these are.)

Amateur investors who attempt to beat the odds on high-risk investments do nothing but feed more money into the pockets of the professionals. The brokers on the commodities and stock exchanges make money whether the investors do or not. They make it when their clients buy and then again when they sell. It matters naught whether the investors make or lose money on the transactions (as far as commissions are concerned). It would be great if a brokerage house would agree to forgo all commissions if the products they sell don't return a profit, but it doesn't work that way.

Over the years I have seen some very good investments and some very bad ones. It is impossible to categorize any single investment absolutely. Someone with specialized abilities can take a risky investment and make it less risky because of his or her knowledge and ability. As it will be throughout this book, my analysis of risk is based on the average, nonprofessional investor. If you are a thoroughly professional investor and average 25 percent a year return on your capital, you probably wasted some of it on this book. If you think you are a professional investor and average less than 25 percent a year return, you're probably fooling yourself, so read on.

WORST INVESTMENT #1: COMMODITIES SPECULATION

Commodities trading is the buying and selling of materials for future delivery. Perhaps the best book ever written on this subject for the average investor is *God in the Pits* by Mark Ritchie, a professional commodities trader in Chicago. Mark is a Christian and a good friend, and is clearly one of the most successful commodities traders in America.

In chapter 1 of his book Mark describes the details of how the Hunt fortune was lost through speculative trading in the silver futures market. That one story should be frightening enough to convince any novice with less than $5 billion that commodities trading is not for the sane investor.

I have known Mark for many years, so I think I understand the mentality of what it takes to be a Christian in the commodities business. Unless you have the absolute conviction that everything you own belongs to God (literally) and can go to bed at night with the understanding that everything you have worked for most of your life can be lost while you sleep, don't trade commodities.

In the past several years, as the commodities business has become less attractive to the average investor, many speculators have shifted to trading in option contracts. An option contract gives an investor the right to purchase a futures contract at a future date. If that doesn't confuse you, nothing will.

Basically, it means that, as an investor, you pay a fee for the right to buy a contract at a future date. If the material goes up while you hold the option, you may elect to exercise the option and purchase the contract. More commonly, the option itself is resold at a profit.

The other side of options is that if prices decline you can elect to drop the option, forfeiting the option money. The advantage of options, as opposed to an actual futures contract, is that the downside risk is the amount you have paid for the option. In a futures contract the risk is potentially much greater.

Allow me to illustrate. Let's assume you purchase a

futures contract to deliver soybeans in 90 days at $5 per bushel, and they are presently selling for $4 a bushel. A smart investor would buy a contract for 1,000 bushels to be delivered in 90 days at $5, and immediately purchase 1,000 bushels at market price for $4. You just made $1,000 and all you have to do is store the beans for 90 days; it's a good deal. But what if in three months soybeans are down to $3 a bushel? In that case you will have just lost $1,000.

The losses can be greatly magnified through credit. Suppose you bought the contract on margin (credit) and put down 50 percent. If soybeans go to $5 a bushel, you stand to make more than 300 percent in 90 days. If they go to $3, you can lose the same percentage! The risk is high, but so are the potential profits. If they weren't, who would be foolish enough to risk money?

Commodities trading does have an honorable purpose, though it has been lost in the mad dash for instant riches. The commodities exchange was created to provide a method for farmers to presell their crops, thus assuring them a variable, but guaranteed, price each season. However, a quick check of the volume traded on the commodities exchange reveals that many more future delivery contracts are sold than crops are grown. What that obviously means is that many commodities contracts are never meant for delivery. They are paper transactions, designed and used only for speculation.

Trying to guess the future prices of agricultural commodities can be a stressful way to earn a living. I recall when the fighting between England and Argentina erupted over the Falkland Islands several years ago, the common logic was that soybean prices would skyrocket since Argentina was a major producer of that commodity. But, contrary to logic, after the English launched their attack the price of soybeans went down limit (the maximum allowed by the exchange in a single day's trading). Those speculators who guessed wrong, including my friend Mark, found themselves unable to sell their contracts. That's known as "catching a financial alligator." They're a lot easier to catch than to let go. Mark suffered his losses and survived, but I'm sure there were many others who lost a lifetime of earnings.

When the Gulf War broke out in January 1991, the same anomaly happened with oil. The common consensus was that oil prices would skyrocket to around $40 per barrel. Those who purchased future delivery contracts at the prevailing $26-per-barrel rate at the outbreak of the war saw prices plummet to nearly $20. That's called "wipe out."

There are ways to reduce the overall risk in commodities, such as buying options. But even so, this merely limits the downside risk. It does not reduce the risk of losing your investment money. My advice to anyone who does not own a seat on the Chicago Board of Trade is: Stay out of the commodities business. And to those who do own seats on the board: Sell them and get an honest job.

WORST INVESTMENT #2:
PARTNERSHIPS

Contrary to some teachers in Christian circles, I do not believe the Bible prohibits Christians from being in partnerships. The admonition against partnerships with nonbelievers in 2 Corinthians 6:14-15 is clear but does not extend beyond that.

Having made the point that partnerships between believers are allowable, in no way do I mean to imply that they are advisable—especially financial partnerships.

The Apostle Paul wrote to the Corinthians that "all things are lawful for me, but not all things are profitable" (1 Corinthians 6:12). That is a very good principle to bear in mind. The Lord told Peter that he should "kill and eat" (Acts 10:13). The instructions were clear that all foods and animals were allowable to eat. I would assume that would include buzzards and skunks, but they wouldn't be too palatable.

In the investment arena the most common financial partnerships are "limited partnerships," meaning that the contractual arrangement specifies a "general" or managing partner, and one or more non-managing or "limited" partners.

The intent of a limited partnership is to limit the liability of the non-managing partners to their financial investments only. Thus they would be sheltered from lawsuits, contract defaults, and future losses.

Based on observation I have often wondered if the "limited" in limited partnerships means that a participant is limited in his or her ability to get back the money invested.

Some limited partnerships require future financial participation in the event of operating losses or specified capital infusions, so they aren't all that limited. But even the limited partnerships that specify no future financial obligations have one hidden flaw — recapture.

Recapture is a nasty rule practiced by the IRS that says: When a property is sold or foreclosed, some or all of the previous tax deferments become due and payable, and the forfeiture of any outstanding debt becomes "phantom" income. The income may be "phantom," but the taxes aren't. They are due and payable when the loan is transferred back to the lender.

Understanding tax deferment is crucial when investing in any partnership that provides a tax write-off. There are virtually no tax eliminations where the IRS is concerned. True tax eliminations are things like tax credits, personal exemptions, operating losses, and such. All other tax reductions are called deferments, meaning that they are delayed until the investments are sold or otherwise transferred. It's the "otherwise" that has gotten many unknowledgeable investors into trouble.

Allow me to share a typical horror story involving a limited partnership. A Christian I'll call Henry developed some limited partnerships to invest in apartment complexes. He was particularly good at taking complexes that were losing money and turning them around. The limited partners were required to invest enough money to renovate the complexes and provide enough operating capital to carry the complexes until they could be rented. There was nothing wrong with Henry's investment philosophy and, based on an estimated five-year holding period before the complexes were resold, the average return to the investors was over 50 percent a year! With that kind of return there was no lack of willing investors.

Some of the complexes were particularly desirable income properties. These were kept for income rather than sold. As the properties appreciated in value, the general partner, Henry, borrowed the original investment capital (and then some) out of the complexes and returned it to the partners. Effectively the investors had an appreciating asset that generated good income in which they had virtually no money. That's a good deal by any investment standard.

When a complex was sold the partners knew they would have capital gains taxes to pay as well as some recapture of depreciation write-offs, depending on how long the complex had been held. Since they made a sizable profit from the sale, it was no difficulty to pay the taxes. But an event occurred that was ultimately to shatter the bubble of high returns with low risk.

In 1986 President Ronald Reagan proposed the most sweeping changes in the tax laws since the late sixties. One of the changes was to disallow tax write-offs from passive income investments (such as apartment complexes) against earned income. This meant that many high-income investors, who bought properties and used the depreciation to shelter their regular income, lost that capability. The result was an almost instant collapse of limited partnerships in general, and income property partnerships in particular. Basically there were virtually no buyers for apartment complexes that were developed to shelter taxes.

Even worse, new complexes under construction were dumped on the market at drastic discounts. Investors backed out of many new complexes and desperate mortgage lenders hired managers to rent them out at far below the going market rates. Complexes that had previously been profitable suddenly became money losers.

Many of Henry's complexes fell into arrears and were foreclosed by the lenders. Each complex that was foreclosed carried with it a tax liability for the accumulated depreciation and forgiveness of debt. The outstanding debt was considered as income to the partners when the mortgage companies reassumed the liability. The partners found themselves faced with hundreds of thousands of dollars in tax liabilities and no money to pay them.

Many limited partners, whom I know personally, will be repaying their taxes for several years at substantial interest rates. Their homes are attached as collateral and several have had their personal assets sold at public auction. Their liability was not as limited as they had been led to believe.

WORST INVESTMENT #3:
TAX SHELTERS

Although this category includes some of the other all-time worst investments, such as the limited partnerships just described, I decided to list it separately because it is a great way to lose everything you have and then some.

Tax shelter investments are in a category by themselves simply because they are used primarily to defer income taxes rather than for any economic value they might have. It does not mean that they have no economic value. Any investment that has no economic value is prohibited, according to tax law. But if the intent is primarily the deferment of current tax liability, then I would classify that investment as a tax shelter.

Since the 1986 Tax Reform Act, tax shelters for the average investor have been much curtailed. As noted earlier, passive investment tax benefits cannot be used to shelter earned income (in most cases). Therefore, it is usually the investor with significant passive income who is attracted to existing tax shelters.

But since all things that go around come around, tax shelters for the average investor will return; of that I have no doubt. In the meantime, there are still sufficient numbers of shelters being peddled to attract the gullible.

As you might guess, I am somewhat negative about tax shelters as investments. The reason is simple enough: I have known many fine people who have lost virtually everything they owned as a result of them. About the only people who have regularly made money from tax shelters are the salespeople, attorneys, and accountants.

Tax shelter investments prey on the uninformed and

the greedy (my opinion). The simple truth is that unless you are willing to spend years in court and lots of money on accountants and attorneys, you will not beat the IRS at their own game for two basic reasons: One, they can use your own money to fight you. Two, they have the ability to change the rules in the middle of the game.

I can think of a hundred personal examples of people I have known who thought they could "beat the system." But in the interest of time and space I will share only one.

A Christian professional athlete whom I'll call Bob was being counseled by a "Christian" investment advisor on how best to maximize his income during his professional career. Bob was a fairly typical pro football player — though intelligent and skilled at his sport, he had practically no business experience. His salary of nearly $200,000 a year seemed enormous when compared to the pittance he and his wife had been living on in college. But after paying his taxes, tithes, normal living expenses, and additional in-season living expenses, he had less than $10,000 a year left over to invest.

Unfortunately for Bob, his investment advisor followed a strategy of using multiple tax shelters to save as much tax as possible and then using the tax money to invest for the future.

He put Bob into a Brazilian opal mine that would shelter $10 in taxes for every $1 invested (using leveraged notes payable). Next he suggested Treasury bill straddles (if you don't know what these are you're better off). These provided an artificial loss at the end of each tax year. Finally, he put Bob into a highly leveraged equipment leasing deal that would shelter nearly $20 in taxes for every $1 invested (again using future debt and investment tax credits).

The result was that Bob saved all of his tax liability (federal and state). This provided him with an additional $70,000 a year to invest (less the $30,000 it took to invest in the tax shelters). Bob was convinced that his advisor was a wizard.

The advisor then helped Bob invest in several real estate and business deals for which the advisor received a commission. He also had received either commissions or finder's fees for placing Bob in the tax shelters. I always thought it interesting that during this time the advisor did not invest in any of these tax shelters himself, although he did risk some money in the more traditional investments.

Bob retired from professional football in 1984, expecting to be able to live off of his investments and whatever income he could earn as a teacher and coach. Instead he got the biggest shock of his life: a letter from the IRS stating that he was being audited.

The audit quickly progressed from bad to nasty, with the agent recommending that the IRS disallow all of the tax shelters. He further recommended that 50 percent penalties be assessed, along with interest.

Bob quickly hired a tax attorney to represent him before the IRS. After investigating the shelters, the attorney recommended that Bob plead for mercy. It seems that in the case of the T-bill straddles the investment company hadn't even bothered to make the trades each year. They just sent a falsified report to Bob's accountant. Even if they had made the trades the IRS would have disallowed the deduction as a sham transaction, but in this case there was no defense — not even ignorance.

When the dust settled, Bob owed more than $200,000 in taxes, interest, and penalties, with the interest clock continuing to tick.

Unfortunately, Bob's money was gone by then. He couldn't get his investment money back, and the tax shelter companies had folded and fled into the night. Bob lost his home, cars, investments, and even had his retirement account with the NFL attached for taxes. He now works a full-time job, with the IRS receiving nearly one fourth of his total take-home pay.

WORST INVESTMENT #4:
PRECIOUS METALS

I know I'm going to irritate some friends who believe in precious metals as investments. But I have to say what I believe and, thus far, most of the people I know who have made money on precious metals are those who sell them.

There are two basic reasons why people invest in precious metals such as gold and silver. The first, as with any other commodity, is to speculate on their rise and fall. The second is as a hedge against a future collapse of the economy and/or the currency system.

One negative aspect of speculating in precious metals is the cost of buying and selling them. Unlike stocks and bonds, which have a well-organized and highly competitive market, precious metals have no such market. Investors can buy contracts for future delivery of precious metals in the commodities exchange, just as for virtually any commodity, but buying the actual metal is limited to a relatively few traders around the country.

These traders or dealers mark up the metals, usually from 5 to as much as 12 percent, when they sell them. Then when they repurchase the metals they make an additional premium by way of a discount from the quoted retail price. Essentially investors buy at retail and resell at wholesale. It takes a significant rise in price to make up the fees.

I know there are individual exceptions to this rule, but discount brokers and buyers are not available to the average precious metal investor.

In the case where an investor is buying precious metals as a hedge against a potential economic disaster, there is some justification for not listing them among the "worst" investments. After all, we haven't had a real depression since the thirties, so we don't know how metals will fare. So in fairness to those who sell gold and silver as a hedge against a collapse, I will downgrade my evaluation to merely a "questionable" investment.

Those who bought gold at $30 an ounce and saw it

climb to over $500 an ounce in the seventies would probably disagree. But again, for the average investor who bought in after that one spectacular event, the trend has been level—to down.

Even the most enthusiastic precious metals advocates rarely defend the purchase of silver anymore. So many novice investors got wiped out in the great fall of silver in the early eighties that most dealers speak of silver in whispers only. In reality the depressed price of silver probably makes it one of the better speculative risks for the next decade.

The difficulty with buying precious metals (primarily gold) as a hedge against collapse is one of determining the future of gold as a currency. Traditional hard money advocates say that when a nation's (or world's) currency gets too inflated it will collapse and people will return to the gold standard. Unfortunately, that theory was developed before the communications age we are in today. It is my strongly held conviction that the next currency will be neither gold nor paper. It will be electronic transfers, regulated and controlled by a central world bank.

If that proves to be true, and only time will tell, gold will be little more than a speculative commodity again. Those who don't believe this could happen need to read the arguments from the thirties that the United States could not remove its currency from the gold standard. We did it because of the desire to put out massive amounts of paper money without the requirement to collateralize it with gold. The same mentality (political necessity) may well divorce all world currencies from the confinements of a limited supply of gold. I am not advocating this reasoning. I am simply looking at the facts and stating my opinion.

WORST INVESTMENT #5:
GEMSTONES

A woman may well treasure the diamond she wears on her finger or around her neck, but it is not an investment. For the average investor the same can be said of most precious and semiprecious gemstones. Most novice gem speculators usually buy high and sell low.

Several factors encourage me to list gems in my worst investment category, not the least of which is the difficulty for the average investor to tell the quality and value of gems.

There are grading organizations that will swear to a gem's quality, clarity, and estimated value. But unless you can resell to the same dealer that sold the stone to you, the next trader may not accept the evaluation. Even if the original dealer does agree to repurchase the gem(s), there is no guarantee you will get the current market value. The market value of gems is nebulous, at best, and is not quoted daily as are company stocks.

In the mid-seventies several large traders pooled their resources in an attempt to create a ready market for precious gems, particularly diamonds. Unfortunately, all that came of it was a dramatic increase in the price of diamonds as the companies marketed them aggressively. Many individuals bought "investment grade" diamonds after being assured they were secure investments. "After all," the salesmen said, "diamonds have held their value better than any other investment over the last 100 years." This was true to a large extent because the DeBeers trading company of South Africa controlled the supply of diamonds very carefully, allowing only a few investment quality stones on the market each year.

The net result of this debacle can best be demonstrated by a gift a supporter made to our ministry a few years back. He bought a one-carat "investment" quality diamond in 1982 for approximately $16,000. It was sealed in a plastic container along with a certificate issued by a certified appraiser.

In 1986 he donated the diamond to our ministry. We attempted to sell it at what was estimated to be its fair market value of nearly $20,000 (based on the opinion of the original dealer). Two prospective buyers sent the stone to be reappraised. The first appraisal downgraded the stone's quality one full point, lowering the value to about $9,000. The second came back two points down, with a value of $5,000. There were no buyers at either price, I might add.

I told the shocked donor, who immediately went to the dealer who sold him the stone. He had a written option to resell the diamond to the dealer at the original sales price at any time. The dealer told him a sad tale about his misfortune with other investors and notified him that he had filed for bankruptcy.

Over the last 20 years or so I have counseled many people who have purchased gems as investments. Some were happy because the gems were safely locked away in their safety deposit vaults appreciating greatly, according to the reports they received annually from their dealer/broker. And I am quite sure that many investors who resell their gems to friends and family do make a profit. But to date I have not met a single novice (nonprofessional) investor who has made money on gems, except by reselling to another friend who didn't know better either.

WORST INVESTMENT #6:
COINS

Collectible coins, stamps, and other unique items can be good investments for knowledgeable buyers who take the time and effort to become proficient at their trade. It is not to this group that I speak. Nor is it to those who collect coins and stamps for a hobby. Basically they don't care if the items appreciate or not. Obviously anyone would rather their assets appreciate, but if they are not going to sell them, who cares?

I restore old cars as a hobby, and I really don't intend to sell them. I periodically check to see what equivalent cars are selling for but only by way of interest. Most of the cars have so much of my labor in them that at double the market price I would net about a dollar an hour for my time. For me, it's a hobby, not an investment.

Several companies offer numismatic (collectible)

coins as investments. In the eighties collectible coins became very popular investments, not only because they could appreciate in value as collectibles but also because the coins usually contained precious metals.

There is no doubt that many numismatic coins have appreciated over the last two decades, so why list them among the worst investments? Because, in general, it is the professional collector who has done well, not the novice investor. In recent years many trade shows have developed to buy and sell coins. These establish a market for coins and have helped to standardize the pricing through a very detailed grading system between traders.

But if the market for collectible coins were limited to dealers only, the prices would quickly settle down with little or no appreciation. Why? Because the traders would all know the true value of the coins and would not sell too low or buy too high (except for extreme cases of hardship).

For the price spiral to continue, it is necessary to market the coins to the general public. Thus a trader buys coins at their true market value at a show, then resells them to investors (usually through a recruited mailing list) at higher prices. If enough investors can be found, the dealer makes his own market.

If a novice investor attempts to resell a coin at the listed market price, he quickly discovers that what he paid was retail and the price he is offered is wholesale. The dealer buys low and sells high, so the investor is forced to resell to the dealer at a substantial discount.

If dealers would make their mailing lists available (which they won't), investors might be able to command dealer prices. Some dealers will offer to resell your coins or even repurchase them at the wholesale price. But unless the coins have appreciated greatly, you end up either losing some of your investment or, at best, making a small gain. Again, drawing on the testimonies of many people I have counseled who purchased coins for investment purposes, the vast majority said they lost money; some of them, a lot of money!

If you're not interested in studying numismatic coins, you'll probably find they are not a good investment for you. One side note is necessary here. If you ask friends who bought coins, they will probably tell you they did well. That's because, compared to some of the other investments they made, the coins lost the least. That is not exactly what you're looking for from your investments.

WORST INVESTMENT #7:
STOCKS

Since I have already alienated a large number of my friends who sell investments, I figure that I might as well go the whole way and irritate the rest — so I have included stocks among my worst investments list.

Again, I would emphasize that a knowledgeable, professional investor can and does make money regularly on common stocks. Also, anyone can learn how to evaluate stocks and reduce the risks involved. But for the average investor, today's market is not like that of our fathers' day. Determining which stocks will do well and which will not is a highly technical field that very few investors are equipped to handle.

I would also like to make it clear that I am not trying to discourage those who invest in a single stock, such as that offered by the company they work for. I am referring to novice investors who buy stocks based on their "gut" feelings. More often than not, what they are feeling are simple gas pains.

If you took a portion of your savings and bought a representative sample of "blue chip" stocks and then just held onto them for 20 years you would do fairly well. From 1970 to 1990 your investment would have kept pace with inflation and earned about 3 percent a year in real growth. Unfortunately, the average investor doesn't do that. He hears of a strong bull market and jumps in, trying to make a big hit. Usually by the time he hears about the bull market it has peaked, so he gets in at the top. Then the market turns down and he sells in a panic to avoid taking the big loss. It has been my observation that the net transaction is a loss, with rare exception.

If you are one of those people who can dollar average your stock purchases, meaning that you continue to invest in the blue chips during good times and bad, you will do okay. But it also means that you have probably just moved out of the average or novice category, in which case you would be better off switching your investment over to mutual funds where a knowledgeable professional with a proven track record will manage your stocks for you.

You may or may not agree with my worst investment list, but I developed it by observing how others have consistently lost their hard-earned money over the years. Some people have beaten the system and walked away with their earnings. But on the average the people I counsel are not professional investors, and they range in incomes all the way from half a million dollars a year to less than $10,000. Some are college graduates; some have not completed high school. Some are senior citizens; others are just starting out. The point is, they represent the average American investor pretty well, both Christian and non-Christian. Most would heartily agree that had they avoided these "worst investments" they would have been much better off financially today. But that decision is up to you. As Proverbs 18:15 says: "The mind of the prudent acquires knowledge, and the ear of the wise seeks knowledge."

 **5**

The Best Investments

Since I don't want to seem anti-investment oriented, I decided to include a chapter on the investments that have worked out best for those I have counseled. This in no way implies that everyone who selected one of these investments made money with it, any more than those who selected the previous group always lost money. But on the average, more people made money using these investments than lost money.

BEST INVESTMENT #1:
A HOME

Without question, the best overall investment for the majority of Americans has been their homes. Residential housing has kept track with inflation and appreciated approximately 4 percent a year besides. That doesn't make it the best growth investment, but it does make it the best performer for the average individual.

It is also important to remember that our homes serve a purpose beyond the investment sphere. A home is something that you can use while it appreciates.

Many investment analysts have recently commented that the boom in residential housing is over. That is probably true to some extent. I believe that the expansion of single-family residences via cheap credit is winding down and housing will be more expensive for young couples. But Americans are hooked on having their own homes. If that trend changes it will only be because the country is in the midst of another Great Depression, in which case all other investments are equally at risk.

It is unfortunate that most Americans have been duped into accepting long-term debt on their homes as normal. With the prices of homes being what they are today, most young couples need extended loans to lower their monthly payments initially. But any couple can pay their home off in 10 to 15 years simply by controlling their lifestyles and prepaying their principal a little bit each month.

A simple investment strategy to follow is to make the ownership of your home your first investment priority. Then use the monthly mortgage payments you were making to start your savings for education or retirement. If you can retire your home mortgage before your kids go to college, they can graduate debt-free (and you too).

The most common argument against paying off a home mortgage early is the loss of the tax deduction for the interest. Allow me to expose this myth once and for all.

Let's assume that you are in a 30 percent federal tax bracket and a 6 percent state tax bracket. We'll also forget that the tax rates are graduated (based on a lower percentage at lower incomes). For each $1,000 in interest you pay on a home mortgage, you will receive 30 percent of it from the IRS and 6 percent from the state, right? ($1,000 x 30% = $300; $1,000 x 6% = $60.) So you will net $360 for your $1,000 interest payment. What happened to the other $640 you paid in interest?

As best I can tell, the mortgage company kept your money and you only received a portion of it back through tax deductions. What would happen if instead of paying interest on a mortgage you simply paid the taxes?

You would owe $360 in federal and state income taxes, but would keep $640. I'm not an investment counselor, but that seems like a better deal to me.

Retiring your home mortgage early pays huge investment dividends. Suppose, for instance, that you have a 30-year mortgage at 10 percent on a loan of $100,000.

The first of the following two illustrations shows how much a 35-year-old man retiring at age 65 could save in a retirement account at 6 percent if the home mortgage was retired early by paying an additional $100 per month and then the mortgage payments he had been making were saved in the retirement account.

- $100,000 mortgage at 10% for 30 years = $315,720
- $100 per month additional payment saves $90,033 in interest. Home is paid off in 19 years.
- Mortgage payment of $877/month + $100/month prepayment invested in retirement account at 6% for 11 years = $182,947 (approx.)

NET RESULT: Home paid off (at age 54, at total cost of $225,687) and $182,947 in savings by age 65.

The next illustration shows the comparison if, instead of prepaying the mortgage, the same person continued to pay the mortgage for 30 years while putting the $100 extra in a retirement account.

- $100,000 mortgage at 10% for 30 years = $315,720
- $100 per month invested in retirement account at 6% for 30 years = $100,953 (approx.)

NET RESULT: Home paid off (at age 65, at total cost of $315,720) and $100,953 in savings by age 65.

CONCLUSION: Paying off the mortgage before saving for retirement nets an additional $81,994 toward retirement (*plus* the savings on the mortgage).

The bottom line is, you're a lot better off financially earning interest than you are paying it. As Proverbs 9:9 says, "Give instruction to a wise man, and he will be still wiser, teach a righteous man, and he will increase his learning."

BEST INVESTMENT #2:
RENTAL PROPERTIES

It has often been said that the thing you know best, you do best. The majority of Americans know how to evaluate rental properties, particularly residential housing. Most of us have been renters ourselves at one time or another, or have bought and sold homes. Most homeowners have the ability to evaluate good rental real estate—at least when compared to buying soybeans, stocks, or coins. Therefore, rental properties are a logical source of investments—but not for everyone.

There are assets and liabilities to owning rental properties. Unless you have a strong personality and are willing to eject some nonpaying tenants from time to time, you need to avoid becoming a landlord.

A friend who has done exceedingly well in residential rentals over the years has a philosophy that I endorse. First, he sets his rent levels at less than the going market rates in his area. This is so he will attract a good volume of potential renters and can then qualify them according to the criteria he has established over the years, which include credit checks, previous rentals, and personal references. His low-rent policy also helps to attract long-term tenants who know they could never duplicate the deal he has provided them.

He establishes his rental rates on the basis of covering his mortgage payments and other out-of-pocket costs, including that of maintaining the properties. His goal has always been to use the rental income to pay off the mortgages, and then use the mortgage payment money for his retirement income. During the first 10 to 15 years he receives very little, if any, personal income from the rentals. Yet he now owns several dozen rental houses debt-free and has a sizable, and very stable, income.

Often he has shared stories of renters who have maintained the properties at their own expense, including one who totally reroofed a home because he did not want his rent to go up. This is one of the rare win-win situations with rental properties.

One of the most attractive aspects of rental property is that the initial investment is not excessively large in many areas. An additional benefit is that once the property is rented the tenants pay off the mortgage for you.

Many investors have moved up from single-family rentals to duplexes or triplexes because the risk is reduced. The chances of a unit being vacant are cut proportionately to the number of tenants it will accommodate. The flipside of the coin is that the initial costs also go up, and often to buy such a unit requires a partnership arrangement with someone else.

One additional idea is to joint venture a rental home with a couple who will live in it. Usually this means the investor will provide the down payment and assumes a 50-percent (negotiable) interest in the property. The tenant couple then will pay the mortgage payments and all other associated costs, including maintenance. When the house is resold, usually after no more than 10 years, the investor receives the down payment back and the two parties split the profits equally. There is a risk that the property will not appreciate, but that is the risk you run with any investment.

BEST INVESTMENT #3:
MUTUAL FUNDS

The whole concept of mutual funds is designed to attract the average investor. The pooling of a large number of small investors' moneys to buy a broad diversity of stocks (and other securities) is a simple way of spreading the risks.

Most of the average-income families I know who have accumulated supplemental income for education or retirement have done so successfully through the use of mutual funds. I particularly like mutual funds because (1) most allow small incremental investments, (2) they provide professional investment management, and (3) they allow great flexibility through the shifting of funds between a variety of investment assets.

As with any other area of investing, you must exercise caution and acquire some fundamental knowledge of what you're doing. There are funds that perform well in good economies and then lose it all in economic downturns. There are funds that guessed right once and basically never duplicated the feat again. There are funds that charge excessive administrative fees and dilute the return to their investors. And there are funds that have performed well for two and three decades and continue to lead the industry.

Even with these, you must exercise some caution,

because their success may be built around the expertise of a single individual. When that person retires or dies, the fund may lose its edge. It is well worth an investment of $50 to $100 a year to subscribe to a good mutual fund newsletter if you have $10,000 or more to invest. It will help you to keep close tabs on the fund(s) you select.

Mutual funds offer such a diversity of investment products that it is probably safe to say that if you want to invest in anything legitimate there is a fund that will allow you to do so. Since we're going to evaluate some of the various fund types that are available in a later chapter, I will not elaborate here.

It is important to note, however, that in placing mutual funds in the best investments category I need to offer a qualifier. A good-quality, well-managed fund fits in that description. A poor-quality, poorly-managed one does not. Later we will discuss how to find the funds that have proven to be the most reliable to the average investor.

Just remember that just as stocks are more speculative than corporate bonds, and bonds are more speculative than CDs, and CDs are more speculative than Treasury bills, mutual funds fit the same profile. So the type of fund you invest in will greatly affect the risk of your money, even in the well-managed ones. The higher the promised return, the greater the risk that must be assumed.

A growth (speculative stock) mutual fund managed by the best advisor in the world is still more risky than a mutual fund that invests only in U.S. Treasury securities.

The question of whether to invest in a loaded or no-load fund always comes up in any discussion of mutual funds. A "loaded" mutual fund means that the sales commissions and administrative fees are taken out of the purchase price of the fund up front. For instance, a $5,000 investment in a fund with a 6 percent load would actually leave $4,700 to be invested in the fund. Additionally, you may also be charged an annual fee that can vary from a few dollars to several hundred or more, depending on the amount invested.

A "no-load" fund means that no commissions or fees are deducted up front. Logically an investor should therefore conclude that a no-load fund is better since 100 percent of your money goes into the investment. That may or may not be true in the long run. If the no-load fund has higher annual fees and commissions, the money you save up front can quickly be consumed in the first few years, and then some.

I personally have found that a well-managed no-load fund will beat a well-managed loaded fund; therefore, that is what I look for. But a well-managed loaded fund is a better buy than a poorly managed no-load. So choose your fund carefully. The primary reason a loaded fund is loaded is because of sales commissions. If you need individualized help in selecting or understanding mutual funds, the fees may be worth it to you. The no-load funds sell their products through advertising, not agents. They will provide any information you need by phone or mail, but use no local sales agents. It is my opinion that a subscription to a good mutual fund newsletter is better than paying a commission, but you may disagree if you know an honest, knowledgeable agent.

As with most investments today, one of the primary difficulties with mutual funds is trying to decide which type of fund best suits your individual need and which company's products are the best. With the hundreds of choices and every salesperson (by phone or in person) totally convinced that his or her products are the best, it can be very confusing.

BEST INVESTMENT #4:
INSURANCE PRODUCTS

I have found in teaching finances on a daily radio program that there is no better way to stir up a heated debate than to discuss insurance. It really doesn't matter what position I take: If I am for insurance or against it (or totally neutral), I'm always stepping on somebody's toes because so many people earn their salaries in the insurance industry.

If you would care to read a thorough discussion on insurance from a biblical perspective, as well as the assets and liabilities of term versus whole life, see my book, *The Complete Financial Guide for Young Couples* (Victor Books, 1989). But for the purposes of this particular book, I'll limit my evaluation to the investment side of insurance.

Over the past 20 years or so, insurance companies

have developed many investment products to tap into the private retirement savings movement. Products like cash-value insurance and annuities have been around for nearly a hundred years, but they were not really competitive as investment vehicles until more recently, in my opinion.

Generally speaking, the accumulated savings in life insurance was, and still is, too accessible to the investor. Therefore, the majority of investors look upon their cash values as a ready source of funds in a time of need. That's fine if the intent is to build a reserve account for a new car, a down payment for a home, or even a college tuition fund. But there are many places to save money at higher rates of interest than a whole life insurance policy. Besides, stripping life insurance of its cash values reduces the amount of insurance available in the event of the insured's death.

During the decade of the eighties, as retirement plans such as IRAs, Keoghs, 401 (k)s, and the like became available to the general public, the insurance companies realized they had to pay higher rates of return if they were to be competitive as investment companies. The insurance companies also realized that the higher yielding mutual funds would eventually pull capital out of existing insurance policies. A knowledgeable investor would not leave money in a cash-value insurance policy at 4 to 6 percent return when mutual funds were earning twice that per year. Consequently, the major insurance companies began to offer policies with much higher yields. With the dual benefit of insurance coverage, plus higher yields, they became viable products for long-term investors.

The two basic types of insurance plans used most often (by those whom I have counseled) are annuities and whole-life insurance (usually in specialized policies such as universal life). There are endless varieties of these plans available. The difficulties are to determine which best suits your investment needs, and then to decide which company offers the highest return with the lowest risk. I have included a chapter on evaluating investments, which covers insurance products, so I will not elaborate on them here.

Generally speaking, insurance products have been among the safest, if not the highest earning, investments. But what has been safe in the past does not automatically imply future safety. The insurance industry as a whole is very sound, but several of the larger companies have made many bad investments. The future of some insurance companies is in jeopardy. It is critical to select the company you use carefully and continue to monitor it at least annually, just as you would any other investment.

It would be far better to withdraw your cash reserves from a policy, or transfer your savings in an annuity, even if there is a penalty to do so, than to risk losing it all.

BEST INVESTMENT #5:
COMPANY RETIREMENT PLANS

It almost seems unnecessary to list company-sponsored retirement plans among the best investments, but it continually amazes me how many people don't take advantage of the opportunities to use them. The jargon used to identify these plans may be confusing, with titles like 401 (k), 403 (b), TSA, HR-10, and the like. But, in reality, the titles simply reference the tax codes that authorize the plans.

The investments available through a company retirement plan are the same as those you might choose personally. Depending on the plan and how it is administered, your options can include annuities, mutual funds, company stock, CDs, or any combination of these.

The disadvantage of a company retirement plan is that although you may be able to select any of several investment options, the plan administrator(s) selects the plan's options. They may or may not be the best options available to meet your personal goals.

One large advantage of company-sponsored retirement plans is that usually the funds invested are tax deferred (delayed until withdrawal). Additionally, many companies offer matching funds based on a percentage of what you elect to invest yourself. Some companies even go so far as to provide 100 percent of the retirement funds. I trust there is no one foolish enough to turn down an offer like that.

There are some potential problems with company retirement accounts. You need to be aware of these and take the proper precautions.

1. *The plan administrator may invest poorly, thus placing your funds in risk.*

2. *The company may reserve the right to borrow from the employees' retirement account for operating capital.* The problem here is that if the company fails, the retirement plan may fail too, especially if the company has substituted its own stock as collateral for the loans.

3. *The company may reserve the right to borrow from the retirement account and substitute an insurance annuity for the cash.* If the insurance company itself fails, then the retirement plan fails too.

Even with these potential problems, company-sponsored retirement plans represent one of the best investments for any average investor. Most companies are run honestly and ethically and have the best interests of their employees at heart. Just be aware of the potential problems and do the checking necessary to verify the solvency of your plan.

Remember, the sooner you start in a retirement plan, the less risk you will have to assume in order to reach your financial goals. Sometimes it is advantageous to invest in a company retirement plan even before paying off a home mortgage, especially if the company matches the funds at a rate of 25 percent or more. It's hard to beat an investment where someone guarantees you a 25 percent return the first year — tax free!

BEST INVESTMENT #6:
GOVERNMENT-BACKED SECURITIES

In pondering what to include in the best investments section I have tried not to get too detailed, lest we both get bogged down in whether a municipal bond from Chicago is better than one from New York. That kind of analysis is difficult at best since risk factors can change so quickly. So I purposely limited the discussion to general areas of investment. Government-backed investments are considered to be absolute security. Among those I have counseled who were older than 50 years of age, government-backed securities dominated their best investments list.

This does not imply that securities such as CDs, T-bills, bonds, and the like are the best performers. As mentioned earlier, they are usually selected for their lack of risk, not their return.

Once you have saved enough to meet your investment goals, whether they be college education for your children, retirement, or otherwise, the shift to government-backed securities is logical. Why leave your money at risk if you don't need to? Obviously your plans need to compensate for inflation, but the ratios should swing decidedly toward the safe side as you get older. Simply put, it is more difficult, if not impossible, for most older people to replace their investment funds; so the older you are, the more conservative you should become in your investing.

 6

The Five-Tier System

I would like to present briefly some of the more common investments available and place them on what I refer to as the "tiered" system (tiered according to how I rate them for risk and return). I trust this will help you later as you consider which investments are right for your plan. (NOTE: This is an expansion of material I have previously covered in my book *The Complete Financial Guide for Young Couples.*)

I have simply assigned a scale from 0 to 10 that can be applied to each type of investment. Zero represents the least return or the least risk, and 10 represents the highest risk or highest return. Therefore, an investment with an income potential of 0 and a risk factor of 10 would represent the worst possible investment. An investment with an income potential of 10 and a risk of 0 would be the best investment. You can't find those, by the way.

I have also added a third factor: growth. Growth means the ability of an investment to appreciate, such as common stocks. Investments such as bonds have a potential growth factor also. If a bond pays a yield of 10 percent and interest rates drop to 8 percent, the bond value increases, and vice versa.

The investments will be divided into the five basic tiers:

Tier 1. *Secure Income:* Selected because it generates cash with very little risk.

Tier 2. *Long-Term:* Selected for stability of earnings for one-year deposits or longer.

Tier 3. *Growth Investments:* Selected primarily for long-term appreciation.

Tier 4. *Speculative:* A mix between growth and speculation.

Tier 5. *High-Risk:* Selected for their volatility and maximum growth potential.

Remember that the rating for each type of investment is purely my evaluation. It should not be accepted as an absolute. Times and economic conditions constantly change, and the degree of return or risk for most types of investments will change with the economy. When interest rates and inflation are high, real property, residential housing, apartment complexes, or office buildings generally do well. But when interest rates and inflation are down, stocks and bonds generally do well.

TIER 1: SECURE INCOME INVESTMENTS

Government Securities — Income 5; Growth 0; Risk 1
Treasury bills (T-bills), Government National Mortgage Association bonds (Ginnie Maes), and savings bonds fall into this category.

Bank Securities — Income 5; Growth 0; Risk 3-4
One advantage of bank investments, such as savings accounts, CDs, and insured money funds, is that you can invest with smaller amounts of money. The disadvantages are that they offer little or no growth because the payout is fixed; and the income is taxable as it is earned.

TIER 2: LONG-TERM INCOME INVESTMENTS

Municipal Bonds — Income 5; Growth 0; Risk 7-8
These are bonds issued by a local municipality, usually a larger city. Most or all of the income from such bonds is exempt from federal income tax (and state income tax in the state where they are issued).

The liabilities of municipal bonds are (1) they have low yields; (2) they normally require a large initial investment; and (3) they are illiquid, meaning that if you have to sell them, you will normally do so at a loss.

Mortgages — Income 8; Growth 0; Risk 3-4

A mortgage is a contract to lend someone money to buy a home or other real property. Mortgage repurchase agreements are commonly offered by commercial lenders who want to resell loans they have made. The seller normally discounts the mortgage to yield from 1 to 3 percent above prevailing interest rates.

The risk on this type of investment is relatively low because you have real property backing the loan. If a borrower fails to pay, you can foreclose on the property. The liabilities are: (1) they are hard to find; (2) the return on your investment is 100 percent taxable; (3) there is no growth on your principal, unless interest rates drop; and (4) your money will usually be tied up for a period of 15 to 20 years.

Second mortgages usually yield a higher return, but there is an equivalent higher risk, including the fact that in case the borrower defaults it is more difficult to foreclose.

Corporate Bonds — Income 6-8; Growth 0-3; Risk 5-6

A corporate bond is a note issued by a corporation to finance its operation. Quality bonds often yield 2 to 3 percent higher interest rates than an equivalent CD or T-bill. Bonds are rated from a low of C to a high of AAA. The higher the rating the lower the rate of return, but the risk is lower as well. One liability of corporate bonds is that repayment depends on the success of *one* company. Also, the income is totally taxable.

Insurance Annuities — Income 3-4; Growth 0; Risk 5-6
This investment requires a prescribed amount of money to be paid into the annuity, and then the issuing insurance company promises a monthly income after retirement age. The advantages of annuities are that the earnings accumulate, tax deferred, until you retire; you can usually get your money out if you need to (although there is often a penalty); and, compared to other tax-sheltered investments, the returns are good.

But be aware that the stated yield of an insurance annuity isn't necessarily what you will receive. Ask for a net figure that doesn't include administrative and other costs; and get all quotes in writing.

Stock Dividends — Income 4-5; Growth 0-10; Risk 6-7
Common stocks usually pay dividends based on the earnings of the company. One advantage is that stocks can be purchased for relatively small amounts of money. It's possible to invest in a stock paying a dividend of 7 to 8 percent and invest less than $100. This obviously appeals to the small investor. Since the dividend is totally related to the success of the issuing company, I would look for a company that has paid dividends for many years, particularly during economic hard times. Be aware, though, that just because a corporation has paid dividends for decades doesn't necessarily mean that it can continue to do so.

As stated previously, a good quality mutual fund can lessen the risk while achieving the same results. Professional management, together with broad diversification, provide a great advantage.

Money Funds — Income 4-5; Growth 0; Risk 2-8
Money funds are the pooled funds of many people used to purchase short-term securities. These are not true savings accounts, but are short-term mutual funds that pay interest. Shares normally sell for $1 each but can vary, depending on the fund's assets value. Money funds are available through most brokerage firms, savings and loans, and banks; those offered by brokerage firms are not federally insured against losses. The interest rates are normally adjusted monthly.

It is extremely important to verify the rating of any money fund frequently. If the rating drops below an "A," remove your money and select another fund. Also, don't maintain more than $25,000 or 10 percent of your assets (whichever is lower) in any one money fund.

TIER 3: GROWTH INVESTMENTS
This tier is in the middle and represents the crossover from conservative to speculative investments. During one cycle of the economy these investments may appear to be conservative, but then during the next cycle they appear to be speculative.

Undeveloped Land — Income 0-2; Growth 6-7; Risk 3-4
During the highly inflationary seventies, farmland and other undeveloped properties were good investments.

People speculated in land just as they did in income properties. This drove prices up and, unfortunately, tempted even farmers to speculate.

The eighties saw inflation subside and land prices level out. Consequently, raw land prices also fell. Today an investment in raw land is considered fairly conservative, although there is a risk if the purchase is leveraged. The prospect of the kind of growth seen in the seventies and eighties is considered unlikely, but this scenario can and will change again as the economy changes.

Housing — Income 5-7; Growth 0-5; Risk 3-4

As noted previously, no investment during the last 25 years has been consistently better for the average investor than single-family rental houses. That doesn't mean that residential properties will appreciate the way they did over the last two decades, but I can see no long-range trends away from rental housing in the next decade. In fact, with the Tax Reform Act making multi-family housing less attractive to investors, fewer apartments will probably be built during the nineties. That should place more value on rental housing.

One advantage of investing in rental housing is that it can be done with a relatively small initial down payment. When investing in rental properties, the most important principle to remember is: no surety. If the house won't stand as collateral for its own mortgage, pass it by.

Rental housing not only generates income but also

shelters much of that income through depreciation, interest, and taxes. The 1986 Tax Reform Act placed limits on what can be deducted for tax purposes against ordinary income, and it's entirely possible that future tax changes will affect real property even more. But I still believe rental housing promises good growth through the end of this century, barring an economic catastrophe.

Negatives to consider before investing in rental housing are: (1) if you don't want to be a landlord, don't buy rental housing; (2) if you aren't able to maintain and manage your own property, many of the benefits decline; (3) it's not always easy to get your money out if you need it.

Remember the three key factors about buying any rental property, whether it is a single-family house, duplex, or triplex: location, location, location.

Mutual Funds — Income 6-8; Growth 4-5; Risk 4-5

A mutual fund is an investment pool for many small investors. A group of professional advisors invests for them, usually in the stock or bond markets. There are specialized mutual funds that invest in automobiles, precious metals, utility companies, government securities, and so forth. In fact, you can find a mutual fund for almost any area in which you want to invest.

Mutual funds are valuable for the small investor for several reasons. (1) You can invest with a relatively small amount of money (many mutual funds require as little as $500). (2) Your money is spread over a large area in the economy. (3) The return on the best mutual funds has averaged more than twice the prevailing interest rates for any 10-year period.

I would encourage any potential investor in mutual funds to go to independent sources and check out the fund first. Since we are discussing growth mutual funds, it is important to verify the track record and projected earnings of any fund you might select. A prospectus from the mutual fund company will clearly define the "secure" or low-risk funds and the "growth" or speculative funds.

I prefer to use no-load (non-commission) funds, because they allow my money to grow without the service fees or commissions coming out of the initial investment. But even no-load funds will normally carry some penalties if you decide to withdraw your money during the first five years.

TIER 4: SPECULATIVE INVESTMENTS

Common Stocks/Mutual Funds—
Income 2-8; Growth 0-7; Risk 7-8

Again, the advantages of common stocks are that you can invest with a relatively small amount of money and potential exists for sizable growth. The liabilities of common stocks are obvious. First, you can suffer a loss as easily as you can make a profit. Second, stocks require buying and selling to maximize their potential and consequently require broker fees. If you expect to make money in common stocks, you're probably going to have to trade them periodically. If you're not willing to do that, it's better to stick with other kinds of investments.

Precious Metals — Income 0; Growth 0-8; Risk 8-9

As mentioned before, precious metals such as gold, silver, or platinum can be purchased either for long-term growth or pure speculation. For long-term growth, buy the metal, put it in a safety deposit box, and hope it appreciates over a period of time. Most people do this primarily as a hedge against a potential calamity in the economy. In an economy as unstable as ours, a small percentage of your assets invested in precious metals can help to balance other assets more vulnerable to inflation. When buying and selling anything, especially precious metals, it's wise to remember what Baruch said: "Buy when they sell. Sell when they buy." Keep a long-term mentality about precious metals — at least those you invest in as a hedge.

TIER 5: HIGH-RISK INVESTMENTS

These investments should play only a relatively small part (5 to 10 percent at the most) in any investment plan. Their primary value is the potential appreciation — speculation. Most generate little or no income and are highly volatile.

Gold/Silver — Income 0; Growth 0-10; Risk 9-10

You can invest in precious metals both for long-term growth and for short-term speculation. This would be most beneficial in a highly volatile economy where major changes were occurring, such as the oil crisis in the mid-seventies or the run-up in silver prices in the late seventies. Obviously, such events are difficult to predict and are extremely risky. They are for the investor with a strong heart and cash only. Unless you are a professional investor, this is probably not an area where you want to risk a lot of money.

Oil and Gas — Income 0-8; Growth 0-10; Risk 10+

In the late seventies and early eighties when crude oil prices cycled up, oil and gas investments were the hottest things going. But many people who invested money in oil and gas did not understand the risks involved, and the vast majority lost their investments when the prices fell and marginal wells became unprofitable. A high degree of risk exists, particularly in oil exploration. If you plan to invest in oil and gas, risk only a small portion of your assets.

Commodities Market —
Income 0; Growth 0-10; Risk 10+

Commodities speculation requires a relatively small dollar investment and can bring huge returns, primarily through the use of leverage. An example of leverage is using a $1,000 investment in the commodities market to control $10,000 worth of contracts — or more — for future delivery. If that sounds good, remember this: "A fool and his money are soon parted." Approximately 1 out of every 200 people who invest in the commodities market ever gets any money back. It is pure gambling. You can lose everything you own, and even more.

Collectibles — Income 0; Growth 2-10; Risk 10 +
Antiques, old automobiles, paintings, and figurines are all collectibles that can be used while you hold them to sell. To invest in these successfully you need to know their value, the best places to buy and sell, and you need to have the capital and the patience to wait for just the right buyer.

Precious Gems — Income 0; Growth 0-4; Risk 10 +
Diamonds, opals, rubies, sapphires, and other stones can be purchased for relatively small amounts of money. For every person I know who made money in gems, I know a hundred who lost money. It's almost impossible for a novice to know the true value of a gem, even with a "certified" appraisal. Worst of all, it's very difficult to sell gems at a fair price unless you have your own market. The rule here is to stay with what you know or with someone you thoroughly trust.

Limited Partnerships —
Income 0-7; Growth 0; Risk 10 +
Limited partnerships are formed to pool investors' money to purchase assets, usually in real properties. Since your investment in a limited partnership is no better than the property and the management, the key is to know the general partner and his credibility. Limit your liability to only the money you have at risk. For most investors,

the risk is too high and the returns too uncertain.

HOW THE TIERS CAN WORK

In a single-income family, the 34-year-old husband is a corporate accountant earning $45,000 a year. His wife stays at home with their three children. They have only $3,000 per year to invest. Goals: to begin a retirement account and to start a college fund.

The family has limited their retirement investing to the employer's matching-funds retirement program. They divide $1,500 evenly between a long-term insurance annuity and a moderate-risk, growth mutual fund.

With only 10 years before their first child enters college, they divide the remaining $1,500 evenly between a balanced mutual fund and a riskier international stock fund for moderate growth potential without a high degree of risk. This strategy should change once the children finish college; then it should be reevaluated when the husband approaches retirement age.

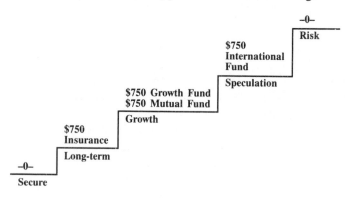

Let's say a 36-year-old physician has an income in the $150,000-a-year range. His goals are to become debt-free (medical school loans, office loans, and home loan), start a college fund for his children, and begin a retirement plan. He has $25,000 a year to invest after making required payments on indebtedness. He might distribute it like this:

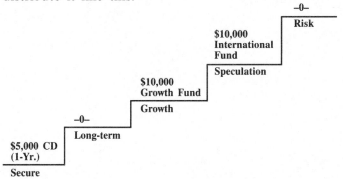

The primary investments here are in mutual funds, divided between U.S. growth stocks and international stocks, for his children's eventual education. Other than a normal amount of emergency savings, his investment money is better used in retiring debt at this point in his career. His strategy should change between ages 40 and 60, then again at 60-plus.

You don't necessarily need to lay out your financial goals in a tier plan. I do this because it makes the examples simpler. The principle is the same whether you diagram or write out your goals: *You need to make very specific plans if you ever hope to accomplish them.*

Both spouses need to discuss their long-range goals and commit them to prayer. Until you do, why should you believe that God will entrust more to you? As Jesus said in Luke 16:10, "He who is faithful in a very little thing is faithful also in much; and he who is unrighteous in a very little thing is unrighteous also in much." Manage well the portion that you now have and God will be able to entrust even more to you.

7

Evaluating Investments

Now let's get down to specifics. Let's say that you've arrived at age 60-plus with your living expenses under the control of a budget and some funds to invest. Remember that at this stage of life you will usually be looking for low-risk investments. It may help to consider this overall view of the options before you.

On the surface, deciding where to put your cash would not seem very complicated. But the competition among banks and other financial institutions in recent years has given rise to a bewildering number of options.

BANK SAVINGS

The majority of American investors still keep their cash reserves in banks. Total cash reserves in banks as of 1991 were nearly twice that of all other consumer accounts at brokerage firms, credit unions, etc. Cash deposit accounts at banks can be broken down into three basic categories.

Passbook Accounts

These are unrestricted accounts that usually pay the minimum amount of interest, while allowing the depositor daily access to the funds. Usually a transaction fee is levied if the account is used more than a few times each month. The only advantage I can see with these accounts is that they will allow deposits as little as $10. Once the minimum amount necessary to qualify for a money market account is reached, the funds should be transferred.

Money Market Accounts

These can go under a variety of titles such as "Golden Passbook," "Ready Cash Account," "Preferred Investors Account," and so on. These accounts were established to compete directly with the brokerage firms' accounts that were attracting much of the small depositors' cash in the early eighties. Some may have limited checking, but most also offer a variety of free services.

Certificates of Deposit

These are time deposit accounts that can vary from three months to several years. Usually the longer the time and the larger the deposit, the higher the interest rate the account earns. Usually there is a penalty for early withdrawal.

A liability of all three of these cash accounts is that any income is taxable as it is earned, unless it is held in a qualified retirement account.

BROKERAGE FIRM ACCOUNTS

Most brokerage firms offer a variety of cash investments, including the resale of most local, state, and federal government loans. Perhaps the most common type of brokerage firm account is the money market fund. These are mutual funds that allow you to withdraw your cash as needed. Many also provide checkwriting privileges. The interest earned by these funds usually reflects the risk they take with your investment dollars.

CREDIT UNIONS

The growth of credit unions in the U.S. has been significant over the last two decades. They usually offer 1 to 2 percent higher interest rates than the banks. Credit unions are now insured by the FDIC, and in my opinion they are probably as safe or safer than banks. If you invest with a credit union, be sure it is a member of the National Association of Credit Unions and is fiscally sound.

INSURANCE COMPANIES

In the past, the interest paid on cash values in life insurance plans was meager but dependable. Because of intense competition, insurance companies have been forced to increase their rate of returns, and this has meant taking on greater risks. As I said earlier, I believe you should look at insurance as provision in the case of premature death, not as an investment.

BONDS AND BOND FUNDS

Bonds

Bonds are the primary obligation of the issuer. The issuer can be an individual, a business, or a local, state, or federal government. Most brokerage firms sell bonds (and bond funds) for a small fee. The interest promised on any bond is directly related to three basic factors: the length of deposit, the amount invested, and the rating of the bond issuer.

It is arguable that some corporate bonds are probably safer than many government bonds. A major corporation like IBM may well be more solvent than a municipality like New York or Philadelphia. Actually a company, such as IBM, is probably sounder than the federal government, although the federal government does have the unique ability to print money.

Usually an investment in a specific bond is for a predetermined period of time. Thus the principal invested is not readily available unless the bond is resold. The face value of a bond can fluctuate according to the prevailing interest rates. For instance, if you purchase a bond for $1,000 paying 10 percent interest and the market rate drops to 8 percent, your bond will probably go up in value. If the prevailing market rate climbs to 12 percent, the bond value will probably drop. The actual increase or decrease in value is what makes the bond market volatile. As discussed previously, it is also what tempts the commodities dealers to gamble on the future value of bonds.

Bond Funds

Bond funds represent the best option for the majority of average investors, in my opinion. The diversification they offer helps to lessen the fluctuations in value and risk. Most bond funds also offer the option of buying and selling the shares without the penalty an ordinary bond would carry. It is important to select the bond funds with the same degree of caution that you would a specific bond. The security and dependability of the fund is directly related to where the fund invests its assets. For maximum safety, select the all-government fund. For higher income, select the corporate fund. For maximum income (and risk), funds made up of repurchased junk bonds, Third World debt, and the like, are available.

Bonds are rated according to a complex formula that takes into account the company's (or government's) projected ability to repay under the most adverse of circumstances. These ratings from the rating services change regularly if the risk of the bond issuer changes. The best bonds, and bond funds, carry a AAA rating. The riskiest carry a C rating or less. For the average investor, any bond or bond fund with a rating of less than AA should be considered risky. Most of the financial analysts I spoke with about rating services tended to depend more on the Standard and Poor's service because of the way they gathered the data on the bond issuers. For an interested investor, this information is available by subscribing to one of the bond-related newsletters.

Zero Coupon Bonds

A zero coupon bond is actually a note issued by a company or government agency at a discount. For example, a 10-year bond with a redemption value of $1,000 may be sold to an investor for $700. No interest or dividends are paid during the term (hence the name "zero coupon"). A more traditional bond has interest-bearing coupons that can be clipped and redeemed during the holding period.

Government Bonds

There are three basic types of cash investments marketed directly by the federal government: savings bonds, Treasury bills (T-bills), and Treasury bonds.

Savings bonds. These bonds are loans to the government for a predetermined period of time (usually seven years or longer). They are considered to be very secure, and the interest earned is not taxed until the bond is redeemed at maturity.

Treasury bills. T-bills are also loans made to the government. The interest they pay is usually about 1 percent less than the current rates earned by CDs.

Treasury bonds and notes. These are usually offered in larger denominations of $25,000 or more, and for periods of up to 30 years. They constitute the government's basic method of financing its long-term debt. The interest rates vary with the prevailing markets, but usually are at least 1 percent lower than equivalent bank CDs and several percentage points lower than the equivalent corporate bonds.

Ginnie Maes

We have noted that these are bonds issued by the Government National Mortgage Association, and they are actually a composite of mortgage loans guaranteed by the federal government and resold to the public. Ginnie Maes can be purchased in units of $10,000 or more.

The single largest negative of bonds like Ginnie Maes is that the borrowers have the option to prepay their loans at any time. So although you may purchase a Ginnie Mae bond expecting to receive your prescribed interest for the term of the bond, if the interest rates drop and the borrower elects to refinance and thus pays off your bond, you have no option. You may well find yourself trying to reinvest your funds at substantially lower interest rates.

TAX CERTIFICATES

A little-known and seldom-utilized type of bond is a municipal tax certificate. This is a lien that a municipality places on a taxpayer's property for delinquent taxes.

The buyer (lender) of a tax certificate is legally the lienholder on the property. If the certificate is not repaid with the accumulated interest before the statute of limitations for tax liens expires (three years in most states), the lender can foreclose on the property, thereby assuming all the rights of the property owner.

The interest rate assigned to tax certificates is usually significantly higher than the prime interest rate. Keep in mind the rule of risk and return. The reason the rate is higher is the inherent risk involved. When you purchase a tax certificate you can acquire no greater rights than the taxpayer. If there is an outstanding mortgage, you must assume that loan. If the property has a title flaw, you will assume that too. It is important to investigate carefully the collateral backing the certificate you purchase. Information on tax certificates can be obtained from most county tax offices.

CHURCH BONDS

I have included this category of bonds because of their prevalence in the Christian community. These are loans made to a church (normally) to fund a building program. Two significant points need to be made here:

1. *It is my conclusion, based on my study of God's Word, that loans to Christians (and Christian organizations such as a church) should be made without interest.* If you would like to study this topic for yourself, I would direct you to the following Scriptures: Leviticus 25:35-37, Deuteronomy 23:19-20, Nehemiah 5:7-10, and Psalm 15:5. (There are several other references about lending without interest to God's people, but these will give you an overview.) Then you must decide for yourself whether or not you believe this principle

is applicable to God's people today; personally, I do.

2. *Church bonds are high-risk loans and should be made only out of surplus funds that you can afford to lose if necessary.* I have counseled many Christians, including retirees and widows, who loaned money to a church bond program that they should not have risked. Several lost their entire savings believing they were helping God's work and He would protect them. As best I can tell from God's Word, He is not in the lending business. When you lend, you're on your own.

JUNK BONDS

Junk bonds is a term used to describe many of the bonds that were used to finance leveraged buyouts of companies during the eighties. They are usually collateralized only by the good will of the issuer, and carry much higher than average interest rates.

Since the demise of the junk bond market in the early nineties, few new junk bonds have been issued or offered. However, many previously issued junk bonds are still floating around and are regularly resold to gullible investors. There are even junk bond funds established for the sole purpose of investing in these highly risky ventures. The high returns blind many investors who are foolish enough to think they can "beat the system."

UTILITY BONDS

The public utility companies throughout the country often finance new construction projects through long-term bonds. Over the last two decades, utility bonds (and stocks) have become the backbone of many investment plans. The advantages they offer are stability and relatively high interest rates.

However, utility bonds are not without risk themselves. Many investors who risked their money with utility companies in the seventies and eighties to build nuclear power facilities got a rude surprise as established utility companies defaulted on payments. Cost overruns and government regulations simply made many of these projects unprofitable. Although utility companies operate under a public utility license, they still must make a profit to repay creditors. Those that don't, can't.

Except for the bonds associated with nuclear power development, utility bonds have been rated among the best investments in America for nearly 70 years. For the average investor, the purchase of a utility bond fund probably makes more sense because the risk can be spread over many utility companies. The evidence of this logic can be seen in the fact that even when individual utility companies were defaulting on bonds attached to nuclear power facilities, the utility bond funds were still paying their investors. It is the simple principle of diversification.

MUNICIPAL BONDS

Local municipalities can issue interest-bearing bonds that are exempt from federal income taxes. Many states exempt the interest on bonds issued by municipalities within the state from state income taxes as well.

Because of this tax-exempt feature, municipal bonds are popular with higher income investors. However, it is easy to be beguiled by the promise of tax-free income. If you decide to invest in municipal bonds, or bond funds, you need to verify the rating of the issuing municipality. Several large cities are on the verge of insolvency and are able to pay the interest on existing bonds only by selling more bonds. This is very similar to a pyramid scheme in which only the early participants can get their money back. We have yet to see a major municipality default in our present generation. But I assure you, municipal bond holders during the Depression saw many municipalities default.

Also bear in mind that if your total tax rate is 40 percent, a totally taxable bond yielding 10 percent is the same as a tax-exempt bond yielding 6 percent. It may well be that the 10-percent bond is a better buy when risk is factored in.

STOCKS AND STOCK FUNDS

I have already warned that trading in stocks (and, to a lesser degree, in stock funds) is highly speculative. Stocks should be used only as growth investments for the preretirement years, or for surplus funds after retirement.

DISCOUNT BROKERS

As stated previously, discount brokerage firms place orders; they do not provide investment advice. When using a discount broker you must know what stocks, bonds, or other investments you want to buy. The broker simply places your order and charges a small fee for the service. Usually the fee is a small percentage of what a standard broker charges.

Probably the most widely known discount firm is Charles Schwab and Associates. This company started the current trend toward a nationwide use of discount brokerage firms in the early seventies. For stock or bond investors who need placement services only, a discount broker, like Schwab, can significantly reduce their trading costs.

The argument for using a discount broker is purely economic. More of your investment dollar goes into the investment. The argument against using a discount broker is that you receive no counsel when investing. In general, the decision to use or not to use discount services should be based on your ability to make investment decisions. If you don't need advice, why pay for it? If you do, the fee should be worth what you pay. The bottom line is, a fee-based broker should make you more than his fees cost you.

BLUE CHIP STOCKS

The so-called "Fortune 500" companies are often referred to as the blue chips (an obvious association with the higher value chips used on the tables in Las Vegas). These are some of the largest companies listed on the stock exchange, and represent the base value of American industry.

If an investor had simply spread his stock investments over the blue chip companies (or the Dow Jones list of companies used to establish the daily index) for the last 10 years, he would have earned approximately 10 percent annually in growth and dividends. There would have been some bad moments when it looked like the market would collapse as it did in the thirties, and nothing says it won't in the future, but overall, stocks were a better than average investment. It is the risk that makes them so volatile for the average investor, and the fact that outside of a balanced mutual fund it is difficult for most people to invest in a wide enough base of companies to lower the risk.

Normally good quality stocks are divided into two broad categories by investment analysts: *growth* and *income.*

Growth stocks are usually associated with newer companies, or emerging technologies. IBM was considered a growth stock in the early fifties. Xerox was a growth company in the sixties. Texas Instruments was a growth company in the seventies. Apple Computers became a growth company in the eighties. In the nineties the growth industry will probably be health-related companies. In the next century environmental companies could very well lead the way.

This does not mean that once a company has been a "growth company" that the stock does not appreciate. IBM is a good example of a company that has seen a steady growth pattern for more than three decades. But compared to the company's early days it would

119

now be considered a stable income company.

Income stocks are selected primarily because of their stable, long-term income through dividends. Good examples of this type of investment would be utility stocks, automobile stocks, defense industry stocks, and the like. Once a company has established a decade-long track record of paying regular dividends, many investors seek them as a means to earn both income (through dividends) and growth (through stock appreciation). Often a company that is noted for its dividend payout will see its stock prices fall rapidly if the dividend is less than projected. On the other hand, a company selected primarily for growth may see its stock appreciate even though the company never declares a dividend.

It is important that you know which category a company's stock fits into when making an investment.

OVER-THE-COUNTER STOCKS

The cost of preparing a company's stock for sale on the national exchanges is prohibitively expensive for many emerging firms. In order for them to have a market for their stocks, the exchanges created the over-the-counter market. Stocks offered on this market are subject to less stringent Securities and Exchange rules as far as capitalization, income, and size are concerned. Basically these are speculative offerings of companies in the growth category. Buyers are presumed to be warned by the very fact that a stock is offered through the over-the-counter market.

Contained within this group of stocks are those often referred to as "penny" stocks. These probably represent the ultimate in risk of any stock regularly traded to the public.

The term *penny stock* refers to the very low price of the stocks, although not necessarily only pennies. When sales in these stocks began, the prices were actually a few pennies; since then the name has stuck. Investors in penny stocks should be advised that the risk is extremely high. These companies come and go regularly, rarely leaving any equity behind. The few that survive can appreciate greatly in value. But very few companies now traded on either exchange started as penny stock companies.

MUTUAL FUNDS

We have discussed how mutual funds pool investors' money to purchase a cross section of stocks or bonds. In order to attract investors in a very competitive field, mutual funds now offer a variety of options. One fund may range from growth stocks and blue chips to utilities, government bonds, and municipal bonds. Most funds now allow investors to shift their funds within a "family" of investments once or twice a year without penalty. This offers maximum diversification even for small investors.

When evaluating and projecting the future performance of a mutual fund, never rely on a one-year performance record. It may well be that the managers guessed right in a given market, but cannot duplicate the feat. A trained analyst can review a fund's performance and compare it with current management philosophy, cash position, and market position to come up with a reasonable projection of what the fund can do in the future.

REAL ESTATE

Without question, residential housing has been one of the most profitable areas of investment for most Americans for the last 40 or 50 years. The advent of the consumer credit boom that began after World War II provided the impetus for real estate appreciation, especially residential real estate. Simply put, more families were able to afford better housing through long-term financing.

The difficulty with any debt-financed expansion is that as the debt bubble expands it gets increasingly difficult to keep it inflated. The people who get in at the beginning make real profits since they can resell their expensive homes, move to a less expensive area of the country, and live on the surplus. But as the expansion continues there are fewer less expensive areas to move to and less appreciation in the existing homes. In a worst-case scenario the price of property drops as new buyers cannot manage the increasing monthly payments.

Once investors progress from residential real estate to other forms of real estate, such as commercial, farm land, and multi-family, the picture gets a lot cloudier. Some investors have done exceedingly well in high-growth areas like Florida and California. Others have done quite poorly in areas where the values rise and fall quickly. The oil patch in Texas and Oklahoma is a classic example of this fluctuating market. In these states, investing in real estate is much like investing in stocks; if you hit the right market you can make a lot of money. But if you hit the wrong market you can lose it all — and then some.

What I would like to do is discuss briefly each area of real estate investing and share some insights from others who have done well.

Residential Real Estate

The general rule for investing in rental housing is that 11 months of rental income must be able to cover 100 percent of all expenses, including payments, taxes, maintenance, and insurance. This leaves one month per year for income, or vacancy. The long-range strategy should be to have the property pay off the mortgage before you retire, so that the income is available then. A second alternative is to sell the property using owner financing. The mortgage payments then become a steady, dependable source of income after retirement.

A drawback here is that virtually no commercial lenders will finance real estate without a personal guarantee (surety). I have already warned of this; and unless I could find an owner-financed home or borrow, using only the property as collateral, I would not invest in rental housing.

Commercial Real Estate

For the vast majority of average investors, commercial real estate is beyond their financial resources, unless they pool their funds with other investors. I have already discussed the use of limited partnerships to do this in chapter 5, so I won't rehash that again. It is sufficient to say that unless you have a large degree of control over a project, you're generally better off pooling your investment money in a mutual fund where professional management is used.

From this point on, I will assume that those who will invest in commercial real estate have the financial ability to do so, and are not numbered among the fainthearted. If these two elements are present (money and courage), a great deal of money can be made in commercial real estate. A review of those who attempted to get rich quick in commercial real estate should be sobering enough to frighten most investors out of the commercial real estate market. I will not attempt to discuss the details of investing in one of Donald Trump's hotels, or investing in multi-story office buildings. If that is your investment strategy, you probably won't be helped by reading this book. I suggest a good book on psychiatry instead!

In reality there are only a few investments in commercial real estate available to average investors. I will briefly discuss some of the more common opportunities.

Storage buildings. Some of the most profitable investments in commercial properties over the last 20 years have been mini-warehouse storage buildings. These are the small rental buildings used by many people for temporary storage space. The initial investment in these facilities is not insignificant. Often the cost of land, construction, and start-up advertising can run several thousand dollars per unit. But in good locations the storage units will repay all costs in five years or less. The obvious key is selecting the right location and analyzing the market carefully, including the competition.

Time-share condominiums. When the idea was first introduced in the late seventies and eighties, it caught on fast. Why should vacationers tie up a lot of money in a cramped motel room when, for a small investment, they could own a share in a condo and rent it out when they didn't want to use it?

Difficulties surfaced as more and more units were constructed and the competition for renters grew so fierce that finding them required large advertising budgets and steep discounts. Since the rental agencies were not going to take the losses, the only logical prospects were the absentee owners. Many investors found themselves stuck with a condo they couldn't use, high annual mortgage payments, maintenance fees, and rental costs, not to mention declining income from their units. Unless you really know what you're doing and can manage your own units in an area where you live, my counsel is to avoid them.

Lease-Repurchase Agreements

A popular concept that was developed in the eighties is selling rented office space to investors. I have several counselees who have invested in these situations and have done quite well. The concept is simple. A developer builds an office building and rents it out to qualified tenants. The rented offices are then resold to individual investors who become the owner/landlords. Assuming the tenants are stable and dependable businesses, the arrangement works well for all parties. Often the tenant will sign a lease agreement with an option to buy at a later date. A good office building can yield an average return of 20 percent a year, or more.

LAND SPECULATION

Virtually everyone in America knows of someone who struck it rich in the land business. Those who don't know someone certainly know someone who said they would have been rich had they just had the sense to invest in land 20 years ago. Tucked in the back of our minds somewhere is this secret desire to be one of those people who owned 10 acres in Kissimmee, Florida before Disney World came to town. I had a friend who owned 30 acres there and profited greatly. But it was purely by chance, not by design. But if you are bound and determined to invest, I would offer these suggestions:

1. *Buy only if you can see a future use for the property that will make it appreciate.* (For example, it's generally safe to buy raw land in a developing community where the property might eventually be going commercial or residential.)

2. *Plan to keep the property until it is totally paid off.*

Don't anticipate selling it before a balloon payment comes due. If you can't handle the payments until it's paid off, don't take the risk.

3. *Buy only if the property can be used as total collateral for the loan (no surety).*

4. *Avoid joint ventures or partnerships to buy land.* Often what happens is the other parties can't pay their share and you will either have to pay for all of it or forfeit your equity.

COLLECTIBLES AND PRECIOUS METALS

Investing in collectibles such as coins, stamps, cards, and antiques is clearly more an art than a science. Yet collectible investing is truly a worldwide market today. Any auction of significance will draw bidders from every part of the globe.

The real key to making money through collectibles is expertise. You must know what you're doing or someone who does will sell you the proverbial "pig in a poke." Before you decide to risk any money on collectibles, I would encourage you to focus on one area (cards, stamps, porcelain), read all you can about it, attend a few auctions or shows, practice with "pretend" funds, and then start small.

Collectibles with Established Markets

Collectibles such as stamps, coins, sports cards, paintings, and antique furniture all have established markets or outlets. Some are traded through auctions. Others are traded through trade shows. Still others are traded through magazines. Some are bought and sold through all of the above. The advantage of having an established outlet is obvious. You may invest in a fine crystal glassware set that has good potential, but unless you can find a willing and able buyer you may not be able to resell it.

If you will invest a few dollars for some of the excellent books available on how to understand a particular collectible, you can avoid many hard lessons. Nothing can replace an instinct for finding the good deals. But there are two things to remember: *first,* the more you know, the easier making money becomes; *second,* in any investment field there are people with whom you will be competing.

Non-market Collectibles

Semi-precious stones have no readily available market, except from the dealer to the consumer. In such cases you must know how to create your own market — say by advertising or selling to friends and family. My counsel is to avoid this type of collectible unless you truly know what you're doing and can market them yourself.

Narrow Market Collectibles

This type includes investment-quality diamonds, works of art, historical documents, and the like. I term them narrow markets because an organized outlet usually exists, but access to it is limited to a few select dealers and brokers. So the average investor is excluded from access to the collectors except by random chance advertising.

Precious Metals

The ownership of precious metals, particularly gold, has become as much of a controversy as the issue of whether to buy whole life or term insurance. What has created the controversy in precious metals is the radical movement that believes the economy will collapse and gold will be the salvation of all wealth. While the excessive debt burden in this country could quite possibly bring about such a collapse, I believe that there is simply too little gold available and too much currency in circulation for gold to become the principal means of doing business. In my opinion it is more probable that the whole world's exchange system will become totally electronic, using no currency at all. At that point, gold will become just another speculative commodity. So I recommend limiting any investment in precious metals to around 5 percent and certainly no more than 15 percent of your total investment funds.

The price of both gold and silver fluctuates wildly. When the demand for precious metals is waning, it seems that gold salespeople use the fear mentality to promote gold as the panacea for all economic woes. But remember that in most instances the metal is being marketed at retail price. And when you attempt to resell it, you may be asked to accept only wholesale price.

An alternative method of buying metals is through a discount broker. Discount brokers advertise in most investment magazines, as well as *The Wall Street Journal.* They will usually sell gold and silver for the cur-

rent "ask" price quoted on the exchange, plus a nomi-
nal commission. Be sure if you buy through a discount
broker that you take physical delivery of the metal. I
have known several investors who opted to allow the
broker to warehouse their purchase. Later, when they
tried to recover their investment, they discovered the
broker had closed shop and disappeared, along with
their gold or silver. If you need to store the metal, use
a bonded, established warehouse.

 8

Following Solomon's Advice

I have a friend who is particularly good at selecting profitable investments. For several years he has allowed some missionaries to invest some of their meager earnings in many of his ventures. Thus far his success rate has been almost 100 percent. Sometimes the investments only make a little, sometimes a lot. But they have always been on the positive side. Most investors wish they could say as much for those times when they have chosen their own investments. It would be ridiculous for the missionaries who invest with my friend to launch out on their own. After all, he offers proven and tested counsel at no cost.

Few people realize that another investment counselor also does this. The best investor the world has ever known (outside of the Lord, obviously) was King Solomon. The Queen of Sheba noted that everything his hands touched prospered. So it would seem logical that if we could glean some investment advice from him we should be able to improve our percentages too. Fortunately, Solomon talked a great deal about his financial philosophies, as well as many other areas of life. The Lord told Solomon that He would endow him with riches, honor, and wisdom. Over the centuries he has been noted as the wisest man who ever lived (again outside of our Lord).

There are two basic investment principles Solomon discussed in Ecclesiastes and one in Proverbs that are worth our attention.

INVESTMENT PRINCIPLE #1: DIVERSIFICATION
Solomon wrote in Ecclesiastes 11:2, "Divide your portion to seven, or even to eight, for you do not know what misfortune may occur on the earth." I interpret this to mean that we should divide our wealth (investment capital) into several parts and not risk it all in one place. This concept was known in prior generations as, "Don't put all your eggs in one basket."

Diversification is essential regardless of your age, income level, time frame, or personality. Obviously those with small amounts of money to invest cannot diversify as well as those with greater resources. But as your savings grow, your diversity should grow too.

It is important to diversify not only into different investments, but also into differing areas of the economy. Usually certain types of investments move inversely as the economy cycles. For example, when interest rates go up, fixed income investments such as current issue bonds go up too, while common stocks trend downward

When the stock market is doing well and investor confidence is high, precious metals are generally down. Obviously there are always going to be individual exceptions caused by outside circumstances such as war, pestilence, and earthquakes. And there are times when it seems that contrary investments are moving in unison, but these are anomalies, caused in part by the complexities of our manipulated economy. Sometimes contrary investments are actually crossing the same threshold, with one heading up and the other heading down.

And, lest we forget that investing is an art and not a science, it is important to remember that people, their decisions, and their emotions affect the movements of investments. For instance, decisions by the Federal Reserve Board can affect the money supply and interest rates regardless of what is happening in the "real" economy. So short-term rates might be increasing at the same time long-term rates are dropping.

A good example that investing is more art than science can be seen in the great bull market of early 1991. Several thousand "program" traders (those who buy and sell based on computer models) received clear signals that the stock market would decline. This was a thoroughly logical analysis of an economy in recession and a pending war in the Persian Gulf. Thousands of these hearty speculators sold "short," meaning they borrowed stocks at current prices, hoping to repay them at a future date with cheaper stocks as the prices fell.

Unfortunately, prices didn't fall. They rose rapidly and steadily for more than three months. Billions of dollars were lost by the program traders whose computers predicted higher oil prices, a sell-off in the stock market, and rising inflation. They missed on all three counts by several months.

But even though such exceptions occasionally occur, over the long run different investments move in opposite cycles. To avoid being wiped out if you need money during one of these cycles, diversity is essential. The principle is simple: Draw from the investments that are cyclically up and hold those that are down, and you won't get wiped out.

I have a friend who retired from dentistry with virtually all of his assets in good rental properties. Then, about two years into his retirement, his area of the country experienced a major recession lasting about three years, and many renters defaulted. Unable to live on the declining rental incomes, he was forced to sell some properties at substantial losses to generate income. Three years after he sold some of his rentals at distressed prices, the buyers resold the properties at nearly twice what he had received. He quickly diversified as the housing market in his area recovered.

In our ever changing economy, investors would be wise to diversify even into some foreign assets that are not subject to the swings in the U.S. economy. Certain mutual funds offer this kind of diversity.

Again, my basic philosophy is: I don't want to have to wake up every day wondering what brilliant moves I must make to protect my limited assets. If your goal is to maximize your profits (and risk), while maximizing your stress as well, you probably need to return this book for a refund and buy one on "no-money-down real estate," or "how to short the market and make a mint." I have known people who have attempted one or all of these. Some are in jail. Some are in hiding. And virtually all of them are dead broke.

In 1977 I met a retired couple who were living on the income from Sears department store stock. The husband had retired from Sears 10 years earlier after working his way up from a shoe clerk to department manager over some 40 years. During the Depression years, Sears had often paid their employees a portion of their incomes in stock, since they lacked the funds to pay in cash. As a result he had accumulated a significant amount of Sears stock, traditionally one of the best stocks in America since the Great Depression.

After retirement he and his wife were able to live quite well off the dividends and an interesting strategy of buying and selling some of his stocks annually. He had developed a strategy that was quite imaginative. Each year in the summer off-sale season, Sears stock would dip in value; then during the Christmas season it would regain its value. Knowing this, he would sell a portion of his stock in the winter, and repurchase it in the spring, often gleaning several thousand dollars profit to augment their income.

Not being emotionally attached to Sears, I suggested that he convert some of his stock and diversify into other areas that were not so single-purposed. But he and his wife had a strong loyalty to the company and forgot the cardinal rule of investing—objectivity. He couldn't bring himself to sell any of the stock permanently. "Besides," he said, "this plan has worked very well for nearly 10 years while many of our friends have lost money in their investments."

There was no way to argue that what he said was anything but correct. The only argument I had was that nothing is forever, except the Lord. Diversification does not guarantee success. But it does reduce the risks long-term.

When discount stores such as K Mart and Wal-Mart entered the retailing business, they forever altered the way chains like Sears and J.C. Penney do business. Sears stock took some swift and terrible losses as a result. The last time I saw this couple their assets had dwindled to less than half of what they were previously, and both were forced to reenter the job market to supplement their incomes.

If you select mutual funds as your primary investment vehicle, they will usually offer a high degree of diversification within a single fund. For instance, most good funds allow investors to shift their money from an aggressive growth stock fund to a corporate bond or government fund without penalty at least once per year. If you are investing through a company retirement plan into a mutual fund, you will normally have this same option at least once each year. Some funds even offer their investors the right to shift to another mutual fund entirely, such as their international fund, with only a small administrative fee. Obviously, asking about these options is an important part of selecting the right investment for your needs.

INVESTMENT PRINCIPLE #2:
ETHICAL INVESTING

The second principle taught by Solomon is found in Ecclesiastes 12:13: "The conclusion, when all has been heard, is: fear God and keep His commandments, because this applies to every person." This certainly is good advice for anyone, but it is absolutely essential for Christians. Therefore, the first thought any Christian must have is, "Is what I am about to do going to be pleasing to the Lord?" If not, stay away from it—no matter what the potential profit.

Usually this comes under the heading of what is called "ethical" investing in our generation. There are investments that can yield very high rates of return with little or no risk. The difficulty is they prey off the weaknesses of others.

One example of this is a whiskey future. There are companies that specialize in selling whiskey futures, just as others do in real estate or corporate bonds. The concept is simple. When whiskey manufacturers brew their product it needs to be aged. Rather than leave their own money tied up in these barrels of whiskey, they sell (more like a lease) them to investors who hold the whiskey for the time required. Once it is properly aged, the whiskey company redeems the futures contract and markets the product. Often a whiskey future will yield from 3 to 5 percent higher return than other "safe" investments. Is it a good investment? No doubt about it. Is it honoring to the Lord? No doubt that it is not.

Similar types of investments can be found in many diverse industries. Pharmaceutical companies that have holdings in foreign subsidiaries often sell abortives outside the United States to kill unborn children. Some U.S. drug companies purposely overproduce drugs that are shipped to virtually unregulated countries and eventually make their way back into our country as street drugs.

I once had a friend who owned a considerable investment in Holiday Inns of America stock. The stock had done quite well and appeared to be heading for even higher levels. But after reading an article about Holiday Inns offering pornographic movies in their rooms, my friend sold all of his stock and divested himself of any mutual funds that owned more than a fractional interest in the chain. He also wrote the corporate officers expressing his convictions.

One interesting side note about his decision is that shortly after he sold out his stock, the law governing long-term capital gains was changed to disallow the 50-percent exclusion for stock held more than six months.

If he had waited just one year more his taxes on the sale would have nearly doubled. The moral: It's profitable to listen to the Lord's convictions.

This issue of ethical investing is one that comes up often in our counseling. There are really two diverse opinions that any Christian needs to consider. The first is expressed by Amy Domini and Peter Kinder in their book, *Ethical Investing* (Addison-Wesley, 1984). Basically their perspective is that a Christian (or anyone else) should avoid any company, or mutual fund, that contains even a fractional interest in any product or industry that would be deemed socially unethical.

In principle I agree with their position. The difficulty arises in actually implementing it. If you buy into a mutual fund and observe their stock portfolio from year to year you will find that it changes significantly. The managers buy and sell frequently to take advantage of changing values. Unless the company has a clearly stated policy of what it will or will not invest in, you may find that they were "socially ethical" in one year and not in the next. The way to avoid this conflict is to buy and sell your own stocks, bonds, real estate, etc., and only select companies where the leadership adheres to your same ethical standards, which is virtually impossible.

However, there are some mutual fund companies that strive to adhere to Judeo-Christian values. A newsletter called "The Social Investment Forum" tracks these companies on a regular basis.

The alternative opinion to never investing in any

fund or company that has even an incidental interest in socially questionable areas is expressed by Austin Pryor, editor of the "Sound Mind Investor" newsletter. He also agrees that a Christian should never invest with any company that is blatantly unethical in its product philosophy. But of investments, such as mutual funds, that have only an incidental interest, he says:

> The average investor's interest would represent only 1/1000 of the fund's ownership. And the fund itself may represent only 1/1000 of the company's stock ownership. To divest yourself of the fund's stock does not hurt or influence the company's operations at all.

Instead, Pryor suggests that not buying a particular company's products may be a far more effective and practical way to influence its social ethics. Also he notes that if you own even one share of stock in a company with whose policies you disagree, you have the right to attend the annual stockholders' meetings and voice your opinion in public.

Both of the preceding arguments have validity and I will leave it to you to decide which is the right perspective for you.

In my experience I have found that boycotting a company's products has a much greater effect on their policies than boycotting their stock. I live in a relatively small community where the local convenience store was purchased by a national chain. Almost immediately they installed a rack of pornographic magazines. I took the time to get a comment form from the clerk, who also said she disagreed with the magazines. I wrote the parent company, and within two weeks received a letter of apology from the company president. A week later the magazines were removed. I doubt seriously if they would have responded in the same manner if I had simply threatened not to buy any stock in their company. But again, each of us has to make an individual choice.

INVESTMENT PRINCIPLE #3:
GOOD COUNSEL

The one last bit of direction I would offer from Solomon is the admonition that good counsel is essential to good planning. As Proverbs 15:22 says, "Without consultation, plans are frustrated, but with many counselors they succeed."

One of my major frustrations is the contradicting counsel that is offered by investment advisors and financial planners who present themselves as experts. It's no wonder that many people either don't try to invest at all, or they simply park their money in low-interest savings accounts. Often they have listened to bad counsel and lost a lot of money, usually on the advice of another Christian.

Most Christians don't want to give a bad report about another Christian, so even when someone asks for an opinion on the abilities or ethics of another Christian they hedge by saying, "Oh, he's a nice guy."

I have also done this in the past, to the detriment of

some friends, and have purposed never to do so again. I will not give a bad report without first confronting the person involved, but I also won't skirt the question and allow someone else to suffer a loss that I could have prevented.

The example that always comes to mind is a Christian who left the insurance business to go into financial planning during the eighties. He passed all the licensing requirements, took the appropriate courses, and even learned the language well. But from the first time we met, through a mutual Christian friend, I knew he was a poor financial planner. He was a likable person, definitely a committed believer, but totally incompetent to give good investment advice.

He had been one of the top salesmen for a major insurance company and was a salesman personified. He made friends of virtually everyone he met, and was so likable they felt compelled to buy from him.

I knew that a friend was considering doing business with him, but rather than tell him my convictions I simply said, "Be sure you check it out with your accountant first." As I look back, that was just a cop-out to avoid what I assumed would be an unpleasant confrontation. Also I thought the accountant would realize the planner was incompetent too. Unfortunately, he didn't, or at least he didn't say so. Not only did my friend invest a sizable amount of money as a result of this planner's advice, but he also introduced the planner to several of his friends.

The investments the planner recommended were truly

awful. They were a combination of tax shelters, limited partnerships, and low-quality insurance products. One of the worst was an ostrich ranch where these large, ornery birds were being promoted as the answer to the growing demand for lowfat meats (and an illusionary market for ostrich feathers). After a two-year attempt to create a "McOstrich" franchise, the project was abandoned, along with several hundred thousand dollars of investors' money.

My friend, and his former friends, are still paying for this counselor's advice. They ended up owing the IRS taxes and penalties for the tax shelters that failed, including the ostrich ranch. The advisor has gone back to selling insurance and is doing quite well himself. I learned a lesson through this that has stuck with me: When you know the truth, say it (in love).

My counsel is, always use more than one advisor, including your spouse. Tell them to be as honest with you as they would want you to be if the roles were reversed.

GLOSSARY

Annuity: A contract between a person and an insurance company in which the insurance company promises to pay monthly payments either immediately or at a point in the future.

Appreciation: A rise in value or price.

Blue Chip Stocks: Good quality stocks, divided into two categories by investment analysts: Growth (usually associated with newer companies or emerging technologies) and Income (selected because of their stable, long-term dividends).

Bond: A certificate of debt issued by a government or corporation guaranteeing payment of the original investment plus interest by a specified future date. Includes: church, corporate, current issue, junk, short-term, savings, utility.

Broker: One who acts as an agent for others in negotiating contracts, purchases, or sales, in return for a fee or commission.

Certificate of Deposit (CD): A deposit account issued by savings and loan associations, banks, and credit unions.

Commodities: The buying and selling of materials for future delivery.

Depreciation: An allowance made for a loss in value of property.

Deferment: Benefits or payments withheld until a future date.

Discount Brokers: Firms that place orders but not investment advice. You must know what stocks, bonds, or other investments you want. A small fee is charged for the service.

Federal Deposit Insurance Corp (FDIC): This agency, backed by the full faith and credit of the U.S. government, guarantees depositors of member banks coverage of up to $100,000 per account.

Government National Mortgage Assoc (GNMA): Called Ginnie Maes, the most popular of government agency securities, available in denominations of $25,000, guaranteed by the U.S. government, and subject to federal, state, and local taxes.

HMO: Health maintenance organization

Holographic Will: A self-drawn will written totally in the handwriting of the person drafting it.

Illiquid: Incapable of being converted into cash.

Intestate: Without having a valid will.

Inter vivos: Between living persons.

IRA: See Retirement Plans

Limited Partnership: A contractual arrangement specifying a general or managing partner and one or more nonmanaging or limited partners.

Mortgage: A contract to lend someone money to buy a home or other real property. The lender holds the mortgage rights to the property until the loan is totally repaid.

Money Funds: The pooled funds of many people used to purchase short-term securities. Not true savings accounts, but are short-term mutual funds that pay interest.

Money Market Deposit Account: Available at banks, savings and loans, and credit unions, normally paying a slightly higher rate of interest than a passbook savings account, insured by the FDIC.

Money Market Mutual Fund: In competition with money market deposit accounts, offered by investment companies. They are short term in nature and invest in jumbo CDs, commercial paper, or T-bills. Not insured by the government.

Mutual Funds: Offered by investment companies who pool many people's money to invest in securities. There are over 3,000 funds to choose from. There are "loaded" funds (meaning that the sales commissions and administrative fees are deducted from the purchase price up front) and "no-load" funds (meaning that no commissions or fees are deducted up front).

Numismatic Coins: Coins which are collectible and appreciate over a period of time.

Phantom Income: When the IRS says you have taxable income from a tax shelter or other investment but you receive no cash from it with which to pay that tax, you have phantom income.

Prospectus: The document that offers a new issue of securities to the public, required under the Securities Act of 1933.

Recapture: When property is sold or foreclosed, some or all of the previous tax deferments become due and payable, and the forfeiture of any outstanding debt becomes "phantom" income.

Retirement Plans: (Tax-Deferred)

401 (k) Named after Section 401 (k) of the Internal Revenue Code, a salary reduction plan whereby an employee may make tax-deferred contributions. The employer may also participate by contributing a percentage. Total contributions are limited to the lesser of 25 percent of salary or $30,000 per year. Distributions prior to age 59½ may be penalized.

403 (b) Also referred to as a Tax Sheltered Annuity or a TSA. Named after Section 403 (b) of the Internal Revenue Code, these plans are available to employees of public school systems and religious, charitable, educational, scientific, and literary organizations. Contributions are made by salary reduction on a tax-deferred basis. Total contributions are limited to the lesser of 16⅔ percent of salary or $9,500. Distributions prior to age 59½ may be penalized.

IRA. Individual retirement accounts are available to everyone with earned income. The maximum contribution is $2,000 per year. There is also a provision for a nonworking spouse, which is limited to $250 per year. IRAs for single individuals are limited to those with adjusted gross incomes of $25,000 or less; married individuals, $40,000 or less; married individuals filing separately, $10,000 or less. Distributions prior to age 59½ may be penalized.

Keogh. A retirement plan for self-employed, unincorporated business owners, partners who own more than 10 percent of a partnership, and employees of either. Contributions are limited to 25 percent of earned income or 15 percent if it is a profit-sharing plan. Distributions prior to age 59½ may be penalized.

SEP-IRA. Simplified Employee Pension Plans can be employer or employee funded. Eligible businesses may be incorporated or unincorporated. Total contributions, including any employee contributions, are limited to the lesser of 15 percent of net income or $30,000. Distributions prior to age 59½ may be penalized.

Pension Plans. These are funded by and through the employer. Employees may be able to contribute under some circumstances. They are formal written plans that have defined rights, eligibility standards, and use predetermined formulas to calculate benefits.

Profit-Sharing Plans. Profit-sharing plans allow the employer the flexibility to contribute funds into the plan only when there are profits. Contributions are made tax deferred. Distributions prior to age 59½ may be subject to a penalty.

Stock: An investment in which you own shares of a corporation.

Stock Certificate: This provides physical evidence of stock ownership.

Stock Exchange: An organization registered under the

Securities Exchange Act of 1934 with physical facilities for buying and selling of securities in a two-way auction.

Straddle: An investment strategy involving the purchase of a call option and a put option, each with identical features, at the same time.

Surety: Taking on an obligation to pay for something without an absolutely certain way to pay for it.

Tax Shelter: Any investment used primarily to defer income taxes rather than for economic value.

Trust: A legal contract to manage someone's assets before and/or after death. Two basic types are Living (or inter vivos) and Testamentary, meaning it commences upon the death of that person.

U.S. Government Securities:

Series EE Savings Bonds. In face value denominations of $25 to $10,000, series EE bonds are issued at a discount and are redeemable at the face value at maturity; thus no actual interest is paid.

Series HH Savings Bonds. Sold at par and the interest is paid semi-annually. Denominations range from $500 to $10,000 and may be redeemed six months after the issue date.

Treasury Bills. T-bills are short term in nature. The maximum maturity is one year, the most common maturities are 91 and 182 days. Sold at a discount-to-face value, the minimum unit is $10,000. T-bills are direct obligations of the U.S. government.

Treasury Bonds. These have the longest maturities

of the treasuries with maturities of seven to twenty-five years. Like Treasury notes, they provide direct interest and are sold in denominations of $1,000 and higher. Treasury bonds are direct obligations of the U.S. government.

Treasury Notes. Intermediate term securities ranging from one to seven years. They provide direct interest and are sold in denominations of $1,000 and higher. Treasury notes are direct obligations of the U.S. government.

Christian Financial Concepts

Teaching God's Principles of Handling Money

Larry Burkett, founder and president of Christian Financial Concepts, is the best-selling author of more than a dozen books on business and personal finances. He also hosts two radio programs broadcast on hundreds of stations worldwide.

Larry holds degrees in marketing and finance, and for several years served as a manager in the space program at Cape Canaveral, Florida. He also has been vice president of an electronics manufacturing firm. Larry's education, business experience, and solid understanding of God's Word enable him to give practical, Bible-based financial counsel to families, churches, and businesses.

Founded in 1976, Christian Financial Concepts is a nonprofit, nondenominational ministry dedicated to helping God's people gain a clear understanding of how to manage their money according to scriptural principles. While practical assistance is provided on many levels, the purpose of CFC is simply *to bring glory to God by freeing His people from financial bondage so they may serve Him to their utmost.*

One major avenue of ministry involves the training of volunteers in budget and debt counseling and linking them with financially troubled families and individuals through a nationwide referral network. CFC also provides financial management seminars and workshops for churches and other groups. (Formats available include audio, video, video with moderator, and live instruction.) A full line of printed and audiovisual materials related to money management is available through CFC's materials department (1-800-722-1976).

Career Pathways, another outreach of Christian Financial Concepts, helps teenagers and adults find their occupational calling. The Career Pathways "Testing Package" gauges a person's work priorities, skills, vocational interests, and personality. Reports in each of these areas define a person's strengths, weaknesses, and unique, God-given pattern for work.

For further information about the ministry of Christian Financial Concepts, write to:

Christian Financial Concepts
P.O. Box 2377
Gainesville, Georgia 30503-2377